Berlitz

Cape Town

Front cover: view from the Victoria and
Alfred Waterfront towards Table Mountain

Right: Cape Town's City Hall

Table Mountain The ultimate Cape Town landmark offers scintillating views in all directions *(page 41)*

Long Street Central Cape Town's trendiest thoroughfare, lined with pubs and shops *(page 30)*

Victoria and Alfred Waterfront An ever-popular harbour-front shopping and dining destination *(page 37)*

Boulders Beach Thousands of African penguins waddle around this pretty beach *(page 58)*

Hermanus Some of the world's best whale-watching *(page 66)*

Castle of Good Hope One of the oldest buildings in South Africa *(page 25)*

Cape of Good Hope Nature Reserve Tall cliffs and crashing waves mark the southern tip of the Cape Peninsula *(page 56)*

Cape Winelands Acres of green vines surround elegant Cape Dutch houses, in the shadow of towering mountains *(page 60)*

Kirstenbosch National Botanical Gardens Home to beautiful proteas, cycads and plentiful birds *(page 44)*

Robben Island This windswept island was used as a prison for three centuries, most notoriously during the apartheid era when Nelson Mandela served time here *(page 51)*

INTRODUCTION

From the first sight of the unmistakable profile of Table Mountain, Cape Town works its way into your heart. It is easy to fall in love with the city, and each year many hundreds of thousands of people from all over the world do just that. Cosmopolitan Cape Town is one of the leading tourist attractions on the African continent, and two-thirds of all visitors to South Africa include it on their itinerary.

The inimitable blend of African, European and Islamic influences that gives Cape Town its true magic is evident immediately, and it is mesmerising. One minute you feel as if you are standing in 18th-century Holland, gazing up at an elegant, gabled building. The next you are in a noisy African craft market, with splashes of brightly coloured fabrics alongside carved masks. Then you turn the corner and stroll through what looks like a Victorian English park, with grey squirrels darting amongst the trees. Further on, the narrow, cobbled streets of the Bo-Kaap echo with the sound of the muezzins in the minarets calling the faithful to prayer.

This cultural mix infuses all aspects of Cape Town life. Township jazz rings out from small bars. Galleries exhibit the best of African and European art. A wealth of shops, craft stalls and flea markets sell everything from antiques to African carvings, traditional garments to designer clothes, and gourmet food to fresh fruit and aromatic spices. Fine restaurants offer choices from the best of international cuisine to the distinctive local 'Cape Malay' dishes, developed here over centuries. People sit at shady sidewalk cafés sipping South African wine and watching street entertainers; expensive yachts dance on the water, mingling with brightly

The spectacular view from Table Mountain

Jazz on the V&A Waterfront

painted fishing boats, sleek cruise liners, and huge container ships laden with cargo from around the world.

Poignant Past

Superb museums chronicle the region's history, stretching beyond the days of the early settlers, European explorers, and even the nomadic hunter-gatherers that first lived there. The exhibits do not merely portray a rose-coloured vision of the past. Cape Town's history encompasses brutality and bloodshed, the displacement of the original native peoples, slavery and, of course, apartheid. There are reminders everywhere: slave lodges in the courtyards of fine mansions; dioramas of ancient peoples whose way of life was overturned by the arrival of the European settlers; the undeveloped land and poignant museum in District Six (see page 27), a graphic testimony to the divisiveness of apartheid.

Finally, there is Robben Island, now a museum, but more importantly, a symbol of hope. The world remembers it as the prison that held Nelson Mandela for so many years, yet its legacy of almost unbelievable cruelty extends back for more than 300 years. No punches are pulled here; the simple, dignified presentation of the facts is all that is needed to leave visitors reeling.

Towering above all this activity, rising up like a benevolent giant, is Table Mountain. It first beckoned European seafarers here over 500 years ago, and continues to enthral visitors. Wherever you are in the city, it is impossible not to lift your eyes to catch yet another glimpse. Over half a million people travel to the summit each year, to be greeted by magnificent views of the city, the mountains and the ocean, and to walk amongst the fascinating wildlife and flora to be found at the top of this legendary landmark.

Rainbow City with a Superb Climate

Perhaps the greatest pleasure gained from visiting Cape Town comes from its inhabitants. The people are charming and friendly, and everywhere you go you are greeted with a smile. Desmond Tutu famously called South Africa the 'Rainbow Nation', and this best sums up the ethnic mix that is Cape Town. The main racial groups are African, so-called Coloureds, Muslim and white. The African population is descended from the Bantu-speakers who migrated into the region from further north in the first millennium AD. The

Walking through Bo-Kaap

Coloured population evolved through the intermingling of the earliest inhabitants: the San Bushmen, Khoikhoi herders, descendants of the slaves from the East Indies, members of African tribes from the north and east, and European settlers. Other descendants of the slaves retained their Islamic faith, and are today known as the Cape Malays. The white population, including the Afrikaners, is mainly of Dutch, British, French or German origin. The distinct Afrikaner identity evolved in the early 19th century.

Cape Town is blessed with a Mediterranean climate, and there is never really a 'bad' time to visit. Though summer (September–March) sees long days of bright sunshine and temperatures approaching 30°C (86°F), there is much to be said for visiting at other times of the year, not least that you avoid the crowds. Perhaps the city's best-kept secret is that the Cape is at its most beautiful between April and Octo-

Vergelegen in the Cape Winelands

ber. Yes, there is rain, but mostly at night, and the temperatures are still mild. In addition, this is the period when the region's wild flowers are at their spectacular best, and when whales migrate along the coast.

Spectacular Setting

As if the wealth of attractions in this vibrant city aren't enough, within a short distance lies an incredible richness of natural beauty. There are mountains every-

Ancient peaks

The Western Cape's mountains are among the world's oldest, comprising sedimentary mudstones and sandstones laid down 500-plus million years ago. By comparison, the Alps, Andes, Himalayas and Rockies are babies, having emerged within the last 60 million years, while Mounts Kilimanjaro and Kenya, Africa's tallest peaks, are a mere 1 and 3 million years old respectively.

where: towering over verdant winelands, cradling picturesque Victorian towns, flanking dense, hardwood forests, and stretching down towards colourful fishing villages or vast expanses of white-sand beaches to sparkling waters teeming with marine life.

Much of this can be explored on day-long excursions from the city. You can follow one of the Wine Routes, through towns such as Stellenbosch and Franschhoek, sampling some of the best South African wines while sitting in a vineyard, enjoying spectacular mountain views. Or walk for miles along empty stretches of pristine white sand, spotting whales and dolphins out at sea and decades-old shipwrecks on the beach, then eat delicious seafood in an open-air restaurant set on the shore. Follow in the footsteps of the elephants which once roamed through the lush hardwood forests of the Tsitsikamma Mountains (along the Garden Route), or spend a day marvelling at the astounding variety of colourful plants, trees and flowers in the Kirstenbosch National Botanical Gardens.

The sun sets over Long Beach on the Cape Peninsula

A Bright Future

More than any other country, South Africa is notorious for its history of racial prejudice and segregation, and the legacy of those days can be seen in the Cape Flats, the desolate black townships where crime and poverty still prevail. However, heartfelt efforts by all sides to come together are slowly working. The average white Capetonian is appalled by what happened and eager to heal the wounds. There is still a great divide between rich and poor, but this is increasingly less along racial lines. Righting the wrongs of the past is a huge undertaking, but the will to succeed is strong.

South African cities, including Cape Town, have a reputation for crime. In order to change this, the government has made huge efforts to improve security in the city centre. Large numbers of surveillance cameras have been installed, and mounted security guards are abundant, both day and night. As a result, crime has been substantially reduced, and a few basic precautions are all that is needed to have a trouble-free visit. Don't spend your visit looking over your shoulder, or you'll miss one of the most captivating cities in the world.

With so much on offer, it is easy to see why so many travellers visit Cape Town and why they find it hard to go home. Chances are, when you leave, you'll be planning your next visit.

A BRIEF HISTORY

Cape Town has earned many nicknames over the years, but perhaps the most apt is the 'Mother City'. Since the arrival of the first Europeans, it has been the centre for the foundation of modern South Africa.

For tens of thousands of years, this region was the domain of the San bushmen, nomadic hunter-gathers living off the wealth of game. Beautiful San rock paintings can be seen around the Western Cape, especially in the Cederberg Wilderness Area. The South African Museum in the city centre has some excellent examples preserved in display cases.

Some 2,000 years ago, Khoikhoi cattle herders moved into the area. Although this displaced the San, forcing them inland, the two peoples enjoyed an essentially peaceful coexistence, punctuated by occasional skirmishes. The Khoikhoi tended their herds and traded in cattle with the Bantu-speaking people of the north, and the San continued to hunt game.

The Explorers Arrive

This idyllic life was to change for ever in the course of less than 200 years. In the late 15th century the great European powers were engaged in a race to find the best sea route to India, with tremendous wealth from trade in spices and slaves awaiting those who were successful.

In 1488, in his quest to discover the spice route,

Ancient rock carving

A full-scale replica of Bartolomeu Dias's caravel in Mossel Bay

Portuguese navigator Bartolomeu Dias was blown off course and unwittingly rounded the Cape of Good Hope in a storm. He continued round Cape Agulhas, which is the southernmost point of Africa, and finally landed at what he named Aguado de São Bras (Watering Place of St Blaize) – present-day Mossel Bay – becoming the first-known European to travel this far south. Today, Mossel Bay marks the start of the famous Garden Route. It houses a marvellous museum commemorating Dias *(see page 71)*, with exhibits including a painstakingly reproduced replica of Dias's original caravel.

Dias originally named his cape the Cape of Storms *(Cabo das Tormentas)*; it was only renamed Cape of Good Hope *(Cabo da Boa Esperança)* by John II of Portugal after a second Portuguese navigator, Vasco da Gama, succeeded in opening up the route to the East in 1498. The Cape of Good Hope became a vital stopping-off point for ships travelling to the Indies from Europe, with the Khoikhoi soon establishing a thriving trading relationship with the crews. To keep in touch with home during the lengthy voyages, letters were left by sailors under 'post office stones', to be collected by homeward-bound vessels.

The land adjacent to Table Bay was first explored by Europeans in 1503, when yet another Portuguese explorer, Antonio de Saldanha, climbed the great, flat-topped mountain. He named it Table Mountain, carving a cross into the rock at Lion's Head which can still be seen.

The link with Europe was to remain largely unobtrusive for almost two centuries. Ships would call in, stock up and move on. The Cape was renowned for its great beauty – in 1580 Sir Francis Drake wrote that it was 'the fairest Cape we saw in the whole circumference of the earth' – but also for the ferocity of the storms which raged off its shores.

Colonisation Begins

In 1652, the Cape of Good Hope fell under the gaze of the mighty Dutch East India Company. Formed by the amalgamation of a number of small trading companies in the early 17th century, the Company had grown in just 50 years to be one of the most powerful organisations on earth, with its own army and fleet. Table Bay was considered an ideal location for one of the Company's bases, to grow food for its crews and serve as a repair station and hospital. Jan Van Riebeeck, a 23-year-old surgeon, was charged with setting up the post.

Van Riebeeck built a small mud fort on the site where the Castle of Good Hope now stands, and established the Company's Gardens to grow fresh fruit and vegetables. (Known as the Gardens, this is now a popular park in the heart of the city centre.) After plans to work the land with local Khoikhoi labour foundered, slaves were imported from the East Indies.

In 1666, the foundations were laid for a much larger fort, and the pentagonal Castle of Good Hope was built. These early years are chronicled in the Military Museum at the Castle *(see page 26)*.

Jan van Riebeeck in Table Bay

The settlement spread into the surrounding countryside, as grain farming began near what is now the suburb of Rondebosch, and, to expand further, some of the Dutch East India Company's servants were allowed to become independent farmers. The land which had for so long been the sole domain of the San and the Khoikhoi became the property of the Dutch, with Van Riebeeck laying claim to an area near what is now Wynberg, where in 1658 he planted the first large-scale vineyard in South Africa.

The Khoikhoi attempted to expel the Europeans in 1659, but they failed. With the subsequent influx of French and German immigrants in the early 18th century displacing them further, Khoikhoi society began to fall apart, and was decimated by a smallpox epidemic in 1713. The nomadic San moved further afield, but were often attacked by settlers. Some were even shot and stuffed by trophy hunters. Many San and Khoikhoi eventually intermingled, their descendants becoming part of what is known today as the Coloured population.

Governor Simon Van der Stel was an important influence on the Cape in the latter part of the 17th century. He founded the South African wine industry, building some of the most beautiful mansions and great estates on the Western Cape. Many fine examples of these supremely elegant Cape Dutch buildings still remain.

From 1680 onwards, religious refugees began to arrive from Europe, including Huguenots from France, who planted vineyards around what became known as Franschhoek.

By 1750 the original tiny settlement founded by Jan Van Riebeeck was a small town named Kaapstad – Cape Town – that had over 2,500 inhabitants. A second port opened at Simon's Bay (today's Simon's Town), providing a far safer refuge than the turbulent Table Bay, where shipwrecks were all too common and countless lives were lost to the sea.

British Influence

In 1795, Britain seized control of Cape Town, and thus the sea route to the East, at the Battle of Muizenberg. Under British rule, the monopolies imposed by the Dutch East India Company to protect its own interests were abolished, and much freer trade began. Cape Town became a sea port of international importance, and the town's cosmopolitan character was firmly established.

Dutch cavalryman, 1803

The Cape was retaken by the Dutch in 1803, but the British regained control at the Battle of Blaauwberg, and it formally became a British colony in 1814. Major companies established offices here, and within a few short years

The Lutheran church on Strand Street, 1842

much of the infrastructure that supported the historic city centre was in place. In 1815, the first postal packet service began, with ships sailing between Cape Town and England. This eventually led to the first passenger cruise liners, and was the start of the long-standing association between the city and the Union-Castle shipping line, whose 19th-century headquarters building can be seen at the V&A Waterfront.

The small settlements around Cape Town started to grow. Simon's Bay became home to the navy, was renamed Simon's Town, and developed a thriving fishing and whaling industry. Under the influence of talented architects such as Louis Michel Thibault and the sculptor Anton Anreith – both of whom arrived as soldiers – houses and commercial buildings of enduring beauty were built. Anreith's fine work is evident throughout the region, with important examples including the magnificent Kat Balcony of the Castle of Good Hope, and the pulpit of the Groote Kerk.

In 1834 slavery was abolished by the British, and religious freedom was granted. This wasn't an entirely altruistic move; it cost more to keep slaves than to pay wages. The primarily Muslim ex-slaves soon established their own close community in Cape Town's Bo-Kaap.

The City Evolves

In the 1860s, building work started on the Victoria and Alfred docks to meet the pressing need for a safe harbour for the numerous cargo ships now making port at Cape Town.

By the end of the 19th century, the little village of Cape Town had changed beyond recognition. The discovery of gold and diamonds in the east of South Africa led to the building of railways linking what was now a substantial city to other rapidly developing areas of Africa, and the streets were lined with banks and commercial buildings, fine mansions and large department stores. The prime minister of the Cape, Cecil John Rhodes, built a splendid estate at Rondebosch, and bequeathed to the nation the vast plot of land at the foot of Table Mountain that would become the world-famous Kirstenbosch National Botanical Gardens.

In 1910, eight years after the end of the bloody Boer Wars, the opposing sides – the British and the Dutch-speaking Boers of the Eastern Cape – came together to form the Union of South Africa. Cape Town became the legislative capital of the newly unified country, a role it fulfils to this day.

The Apartheid Era

Although African cooperation had helped the British to victory, Africans did not benefit from the unification of South Africa. The new government began to issue decrees from the Houses of Parliament in Cape Town that eroded the rights of non-whites. From 1913, their right to own property was severely restricted, and from 1936 they were unable to vote.

When the National Party came to power in 1948 under D.F. Malan, it pledged to introduce influx control, to stop what was felt to be excessive numbers of black workers moving to major cities. It would eventually bring in nationwide, compulsory, racial segregation, initiating the abhorrent apartheid regime.

By the 1960s, African workers were concentrated in the grim shanty towns and men-only hostels of the Cape Flats, forbidden to bring their families to live with them. A peaceful demonstration in Cape Town by inhabitants of the Langa township in 1960 resulted in the deaths of three protestors who were shot by police, fuelling the armed struggle against

Nelson Mandela

Born to a local chief in the Eastern Cape in 1918, Mandela's given name was Rolihlahla ('Troublemaker'), but he acquired the 'Christian' name of Nelson upon becoming the first member of his family to attend school. Politically active whilst he studied law, Mandela and fellow lawyers Oliver Tambo and Walter Sisulu formed the ANC Youth League in 1944.

Mandela was committed to peaceful protest in the early years of his activist career, but that changed after the police massacre of 69 protesters at Sharpeville in 1960 and subsequent banning of the ANC, which led to his formation and leadership of Umkhonto we Sizwe (Spear of the Nation), the military wing of the ANC. In 1964, Mandela was sentenced to life imprisonment for high treason, and he was incarcerated on Robben Island.

In February 1990, President de Klerk lifted the ban on the ANC and Mandela made his first public appearance in 26 years outside Cape Town's City Hall. Ensuing negotiations led to a joint Nobel Peace Prize with de Klerk in 1993. and to the far bigger prize of leading the ANC to victory in South Africa's first fully democratic election in May 1994.

Mandela retired as president in 1999, but – now in his 90s – he remains a popular figurehead with South Africans of all races and creeds.

this oppression. High-profile opponents of apartheid, including Nelson Mandela and Walter Sisulu, were sentenced to lengthy incarceration on Robben Island, a bleak prison located off the coast of Cape Town.

The Group Areas Act of 1966 further oppressed the African and Coloured communities, forcibly evicting them from their homes and moving them out of the city to the Cape Flats. The stirring exhibits at the District

Nelson Mandela

Six Museum are an emotional testimony to the despair felt by the inhabitants of these areas. Finally, in 1972, Coloured representation on the town council was abolished.

A New Start

In the 1980s, Cape Town, like all of South Africa, underwent tremendous change as the fight against apartheid took hold. The strongest anti-apartheid force yet, the United Democratic Front, was formed on the Cape Flats in 1983. In protest against the violent oppression suffered by the non-whites, many countries imposed harsh economic sanctions on South Africa. These proved crippling, hugely damaging Cape Town by depriving it of the cargo ships that were its lifeblood. South Africans were banned from international sporting events – a particularly wounding blow to such a sports-loving country.

In 1986 history was made at St George's Cathedral, Cape Town, when Desmond Tutu was enthroned as South Africa's first black archbishop.

In 1990 the city became the focus of the eyes of the world, when, in a surprise initiative by President F.W. de Klerk, Nelson Mandela was released after 27 years in prison. Within hours of his release, Mandela stood on the balcony of Cape Town's City Hall, addressing a crowd of over 100,000 people standing on Grand Parade below him. This historical moment was witnessed by millions of people on televisions all over the world.

Four years later, Nelson Mandela became the first black president of South Africa, and from the Parliament in Cape Town, began the delicate process of peaceful reconciliation after centuries of racial conflict. Today the 'Mother City' continues to play a crucial role in the welfare of her country, with all laws emanating from the city's Houses of Parliament.

The tiny settlement Jan van Riebeeck established in 1652 is now one of the most important centres of commerce on the African continent. It is home to the South African headquarters of numerous major international corporations, and foreign investment is growing all the time. The cosmopolitan sophistication, outstanding location and relaxed atmosphere of Cape Town also acts as a magnet to those involved in the creative industries. Advertising agencies, filmmakers, designers and architects abound, and many renowned artists have chosen to make their home in and around this beautiful city. The city will also host several games in the 2010 FIFA World Cup. Cape Town, and its people, are moving forward with hope, enthusiasm and energy.

South African smile

Historical Landmarks

1488 Bartolomeu Dias rounds the Cape of Good Hope.

1498 Vasco da Gama discovers the Spice Route to India.

1503 Antonio de Saldanha names Table Mountain.

1652 Jan Van Riebeeck establishes a trading post at Table Bay.

1658 Slaves first brought to the Cape. First large-scale vineyard planted.

1666 Foundations laid for the Castle of Good Hope.

1679 Simon Van der Stel becomes Governor of the Cape.

1680 German and French settlers arrive.

1795 The British take control of Cape Town at the Battle of Muizenberg.

1803 Cape Town given back to the Dutch.

1806 The British retake the Cape at the Battle of Blaauwberg.

1814 Congress of Vienna cedes the Cape to the British.

1834 Slavery abolished.

1860s The docks and harbour are built.

1880 Railways link Cape Town to much of the African subcontinent.

1910 The Union of South Africa is established. Cape Town becomes the seat of the country's legislature.

1948 The National Party under D.F. Malan comes to power, subsequently introducing apartheid.

1960 Police kill anti-apartheid protestors during demonstrations.

1964 Nelson Mandela is imprisoned on Robben Island.

1966 Group Areas Act relocates African and Coloured communities to the Cape Flats.

1983 United Democratic Front is formed on the Cape Flats.

1986 Desmond Tutu becomes first black Archbishop of Cape Town.

1990 Mandela released from prison.

1994 The ANC, led by Nelson Mandela, wins the country's first democratic election.

1999 Thabo Mbeki succeeds Mandela as president.

2007 Jacob Zuma is made party president of the ruling ANC, whilst Mbeki remains national president until 2009.

2010 South Africa hosts the FIFA World Cup.

WHERE TO GO

Cape Town is a joy to explore. The historic city centre is small in size and easy to walk around, whilst to the north the beautifully restored Victoria and Alfred Waterfront area bustles with energy and life day and night. Ever-present Table Mountain provides a spectacular backdrop to the city and even more spectacular views from its summit. As if the city's attractions weren't enough, within a short drive or train ride lie a wealth of natural wonders, including Cape Point, the Winelands and the Garden Route.

CITY CENTRE

Cape Town's city centre is laid out on a grid system, and it is easy to find your way around. Numerous tours and historic walks are available, but you can easily make your own itinerary. You can see most of the historic highlights in just a few hours' easy walking, while a relatively undemanding day's exploring will really give you a sense of knowing the place. Be aware, though, that the African sun can get very hot, so take your time, wear a hat and drink lots of water.

Around the Castle of Good Hope

The **Castle of Good Hope** (daily 9am–4pm; charge; www.iziko.org.za) on Buitenkant Street is the oldest European building in South Africa. This pentagonal fort, which underwent extensive restoration over 1969–93, replaced the original wooden fortress established by Jan Van Riebeeck as the headquarters of the Dutch East India Company. It took 13 years to construct, and was finished in 1679. For 150 years

City Hall, with Table Mountain in the background

the Castle was the heart of administrative, social and economic life on the Cape. Today it still retains an active military purpose, as the headquarters for the Western Province Command of the Defence Force, and the Changing of the Guard takes place daily, at noon, preceded by a Key Ceremony and firing of the cannon at 10am. Viewed from the outside, the Castle is unimpressive, but its merit lies in its historical interest.

Three museums are housed here. The Military Museum relates the story of the early years of the Dutch East India Company's presence on the Cape; the rooms of the Secunde's House, originally the home of the deputy governor, are furnished in the style of the 16th and 17th centuries, while the marvellous William Fehr Collection of paintings, furniture, china and porcelain in the Governor's Residence is well worth a visit. This last building is adorned by the Kat Balcony, with

The William Fehr Collection in the Castle of Good Hope

its magnificent sculpture by Anton Anreith. Free official tours are given around the ramparts, dungeon, torture chamber and armouries, starting at 11am, noon and 2pm daily, and there is a good restaurant and tea shop in the courtyard.

Opposite the Castle, across Buitenkant Street, lies **Grand Parade**, where vast crowds gathered to hear Nelson Mandela's first speech upon being released from prison. A lively flea market operates here every Wednesday and Saturday.

City Hall, with the balcony where Mandela made that historic speech, is on Darling Street. Built in the Italian Renaissance style in 1905, it is home to the City Library and Cape Town Symphony Orchestra. Entrance is free to view this splendid example of Edwardian opulence, with its ornate stained-glass window commemorating England's King Edward VII and Queen Alexandra.

District Six, south of the Castle of Good Hope, was once a cosmopolitan neighbourhood, with some 60,000 predominantly Coloured inhabitants forming a lively community. However, it could not withstand the Group Areas Act. In 1966 it was designated a White Group Area, and all non-whites were forcibly evicted from their homes and relocated to the more recently established townships on the less central Cape Flats. Over the next 15 years, the buildings of District Six were systematically reduced to rubble. Most of the luxury houses due to take their place were never built, so strong was the national and international outrage at the demolition of the original community.

Today the land remains largely undeveloped, and the story of the uprooted residents is told in the intensely moving **District Six Museum** (Mon 9am–3pm, Tue–Sat 9am–4pm; charge; www.districtsix.co.za) based in Buitenkant Methodist church. Photographs, original street signs and written recollections of past inhabitants bear vivid witness to the devastating impact of apartheid.

Adderley Street

Trafalgar Place Flower Market

At the west end of Darling Street is **Adderley Street**, named in honour of Charles Adderley, a 19th-century British politician. He earned the gratitude of the residents of Cape Town by helping them resist attempts by the British government to establish a penal colony at the Cape. Once a prestigious residential area for prominent local families, Adderley Street is now a major commercial thoroughfare.

Don't miss the vivid, gloriously scented blooms in the **Trafalgar Place Flower Market** – and enjoy the lively banter of the Bo-Kaap women as you browse. Golden Acre Mall may have an ugly 1970s facade, but it contains a wealth of excellent shops.

On the corner of Adderley and Darling Streets stands the rather splendid **Standard Bank**, distinguished by its tall dome atop which sits a statue of Britannia. Cecil Rhodes used to bank here. This is the first of a series of important historical buildings lining Adderley Street. Another example of fine commercial architecture can be found at the **First National Bank**, which has retained its huge circular wooden writing desk complete with original inkwells.

A little further along on the left is the Mother Church of the Dutch Reformed Faith, the **Groote Kerk** (entrance on Church Square). Here, the important Afrikaans families of

Cape Town worshipped in the second half of the 19th century, and one can view the enclosed pews. Each has its own door, so social distinctions could be maintained, even at prayer. A church has existed here since 1678, but the present building was erected in 1841. The enormous carved pulpit by sculptor Anton Anreith and carpenter Jan Graaff was originally installed in the previous church on this site. Crafted from Burmese teak, with lion-shaped supports made from stinkwood, it is truly outstanding.

At the top of Adderley Street, the **Iziko Slave Lodge** (Mon–Fri 10am–4.30pm, Sat 10am–1pm; charge; www. iziko.org.za) was built in 1679 to provide cramped accommodation for the hundreds of slaves who worked in the adjacent Company's Gardens. It later became a brothel, and in 1810 served a somewhat different purpose, as government offices, housing the Supreme Court. This handsome two-storey building now houses a series of harrowing but fascinating multimedia displays charting the local and international history of the slave trade.

St George's Cathedral, nearby on Wale Street, was the religious seat of Desmond Tutu during his tenure as Archbishop of Cape Town from 1986 to 1995. From here, in 1989, he led 30,000 people to City Hall where he famously declared to the world, 'We are the Rainbow Nation!' The Cathedral owes its Gothic appearance to architect Sir Herbert Baker, who revamped the original 1834 building. Viewed from inside, the stained-glass windows are particularly impressive.

Shackles in the Iziko Slave Lodge

Around Long Street

Parallel with and just west of Adderley Street is **St George's Mall**, a busy promenade lined with many shops, stalls and cafés, where street entertainers perform for the crowds. Just off St George's Mall is cobbled **Greenmarket Square** (www.greenmarketsquare.com). The scene of many public announcements, including that of the abolition of slavery in 1834, it is now a colourful, busy souvenir market, where you can bargain for African masks, carvings, fabrics and jewellery.

The **Old Town House** (Mon–Sat 10am–4pm; charge; www.iziko.org.za) on Greenmarket Square was built in 1755 as the headquarters of the Burgher Watch, effectively an early combined police force and fire department. This beautiful example of Cape Dutch architecture, once the most important civic building in Cape Town, is now an art gallery, home to the Michaelis Collection of 17th-century Dutch landscape paintings.

Long Street is a fascinating mix of bygone elegance and more recent sleaziness combined with architectural diversity. Elaborate Georgian and Victorian houses with ornate wrought-iron balconies echo the architecture of New Orleans, and minarets mark the mosques that draw the Muslims of

Victorian ironwork on Long Street

the nearby Bo-Kaap. Long Street was once notorious for its drinking dens and brothels, and to some extent these still survive, alongside shops selling everything from second-hand books to antique furniture and period clothing. A visit to the steam rooms of the **Long Street Baths** at the southern end of the street is a great way to unwind after a day's sightseeing.

Shopping on Long Street

Situated at 40 Long Street, the **Sendinggestig Missionary Meeting House Museum** (Mon–Fri 9am–4pm; free) is an oasis of calm on this otherwise bustling road. The first church for Africans, this pretty peach-and-white building, constructed in 1804, now contains exhibits portraying the history of mission work in South Africa, with particular reference to the literacy and religious education it offered to slaves in the 18th century.

At the northern end of Long Street, just around the corner from Strand Street, is the **Koopmans de Wet House**. This elegant structure, with its delicate, neoclassical pink-and-white facade, sits like a doll's house between towering office blocks. Built in 1701, it enjoyed the height of its fame as home to socialite and art collector Maria Koopmans de Wet (1834–1906). Extravagantly decorated rooms furnished in late 18th-century European style stand in stark contrast to the slave quarters.

Further along Strand Street is the **Gold of Africa Museum** (Mon–Sat 9.30am–5pm; charge; www.goldofafrica.

com). It houses a stunning collection of gold jewellery and cultural artefacts from around the African continent, from ceremonial objects used by royalty to smaller amulets carried by traders and warriors. The museum is housed in the 18th-century Martin Melck House, a fine original townhouse dating from 1788.

Next to the museum is South Africa's first **Lutheran Church**. German immigrants had to worship in the Dutch Reformed church until 1771, and merchant Martin Melck celebrated their religious emancipation by funding the building of this splendid church. Anton Anreith carved the wooden pulpit, which was so admired that he was asked to make one for the Groote Kerk on Adderley Street.

Government Avenue

The leafy pedestrian walkway of **Government Avenue**, extending south from the top of Adderley Street, forms the heart of the historic centre of Cape Town. On the left, with the main entrance on Parliament Street, lie the **Houses of Parliament**, scene of so many dramatic events in the turbulent history of South Africa. Tickets to watch parliamentary sessions or tour the buildings are available.

Cecil Rhodes statue

De Tuynhuis, the official office of the President of South Africa, is next door to the Houses of Parliament. Originally the Guest House for the Dutch East India Company, it was remodelled extensively by a succession of governors to become the fine building you see today.

In 1652, Jan Van Riebeeck established South Africa's first market garden to supply fresh fruit and vegetables to the merchant ships of the Dutch East India Company. The 3 hectares (7 acres) of elegant parkland you see in the **Company's Gardens** are all that remain of the original 17 hectares (43 acres). At the end of the 17th century, rather than continue to grow its own produce, the Company granted land to independent farmers and bought food from them.

Houses of Parliament

The Gardens were transformed into a botanic garden for the Cape Town elite. It is a delightful place with exotic and indigenous plants, fountains, shady paths and rose gardens. Near the outdoor café stands an ancient saffron pear tree, reputed to have been brought from Holland in the 17th century. A statue of Cecil Rhodes presides over the central path, and an army of grey squirrels busily darts around, the descendants of those Rhodes introduced to South Africa over 100 years ago.

Beyond Rhodes's statue is the **Delville Wood Memorial**, where Anton Van Wouw and Alfred Turner sculptures commemorate the 2,300 South African casualties at the Battle of Delville Wood in France during World War I. Overlooking this is the country's largest and oldest museum, the **South African Museum** (daily 10am–5pm; charge except Sun;

Shamanic art

The prehistoric rock art of South Africa was once dismissed by Europeans as crude and primitive. Today, it is appreciated both for its fine execution and for its religious qualities – most paintings depict ritual trances experienced by shamans whilst in a state of altered consciousness comparable to a hallucinogenic drug experience.

www.iziko.org.za). A magnificent building with Table Mountain as its backdrop, this is a truly wonderful place, with plenty to interest both young and old. It is primarily dedicated to natural history. Notable exhibits include dioramas of prehistoric life and a four-storey-high Whale Well. The latter contains the huge skeleton of a blue whale. The anthropological exhibits are not to be missed either, including remarkable depictions of 19th-century San tribal life, and some truly superb rock art.

The **Planetarium** adjoining the Museum has daily shows, some specifically for children, providing an excellent opportunity to learn more about the night sky of the southern hemisphere.

Across Government Avenue from the South African Museum you will find the eclectic **South African National Gallery** (Tue–Sun 10am–5pm; charge; www.iziko.org.za). This originally displayed mainly European art, and still contains a number of works by renowned artists such as Gainsborough and Reynolds. However, the primary focus is now on contemporary South African art, and there is a growing collection of traditional tribal work, including carvings and beadwork.

On nearby Hatfield Street, the **South African Jewish Museum** (Sun–Thur 10am–5pm, Fri 10am–2pm; charge; www.sajewishmuseum.co.za) is housed in the oldest synagogue in the country. The history of Jewish life in South Africa is chronicled through photographs, art and books in this opulent building. In the same complex is the harrowing **Holocaust Museum** (Sun–Thur 10am–5pm, Fri 10am–1pm; charge), which documents the history of European anti-Semitism and touches on the Nazi influence on the South African National Party that engineered apartheid.

On Orange Street at the far end of Government Avenue is a Cape Town landmark: the sugar-pink **Mount Nelson Hotel**, the most luxurious hotel in the city. 'The Nellie' has been an integral part of city life since 1899. The buffet breakfast or afternoon tea on its garden terrace is a memorable and civilised occasion.

South African National Gallery

Bo-Kaap

Colourful houses and mosque in Bo-Kaap

On the slopes of Signal Hill, bounded by Wale, Rose and Waterkant streets, is the **Bo-Kaap** (literally 'Upper Cape'), the traditional home of Cape Town's Muslim community. It is a fascinating place, with 18th- and early 19th-century 'cube' houses painted in colourful shades, narrow streets, spice shops, and the minarets of 11 mosques, including South Africa's first official mosque, the Auwal (on Dorp Street).

The inhabitants of the Bo-Kaap are mostly descended from highly skilled and educated slaves imported into the Cape from the East Indies. They brought with them their faith, Sufism (part of the Islamic religion), and a strong culture which has survived centuries of repression when their language, history, and writing could only be preserved in secret. Although the Cape Muslims are still sometimes erroneously referred to as the 'Cape Malays', few of their ancestors actually came from Malaysia. Traders at that time used the Malayal language as a common tongue, hence the name Cape Malays.

Until 1834 this area was inhabited by Dutch and English artisans, but when slavery was abolished, the freed Muslims moved in. They established a community which was to survive even the notorious Group Areas Act of 1966. Under this, virtually every non-white neighbourhood in Cape Town was designated a White Group Area, and razed to the ground to make way for whites-only housing. The original inhabitants moved out of the city.

The **Bo-Kaap Museum** (Mon–Fri 9am–4pm; charge; www.iziko.org.za) at 71 Wale Street is based around the fine house and possessions of a wealthy 19th-century Muslim family, with exhibits depicting the history of the community.

Today Bo-Kaap has an insular feel, and you may feel as though you are intruding. To get the most out of a visit it is a good idea to take a guided tour, which may also give you the opportunity to meet some of the area's residents.

VICTORIA AND ALFRED WATERFRONT

The **Victoria and Alfred (V&A) Waterfront** (daily 9am–6pm, though some shops stay open until 9pm and restaurants to midnight; free; tel: 021-408 7600; www.waterfront.co.za) – or plain 'Waterfront', as locals call it – is one of Cape Town's most popular and vibrant attractions. The Waterfront comprises three basins – Victoria Basin, Alfred Basin and New Basin. Alfred Basin is named after Queen Victoria's second son, Prince Alfred, who in 1860 ceremonially tipped the first rock to begin construction of the original harbour.

In the Two Oceans Aquarium

The city's original Victorian harbour was almost derelict for two decades after the cargo ships it was built to accommodate gave way to the supertankers that now dock at nearby Duncan Dock. Redevelopment of the area started in the early 1990s and has succeeded beyond all expectations.

The V&A Waterfront's historic warehouses and dock buildings have been beautifully restored and contain some of the city's best shops, nightspots and restaurants, along with museums, an aquarium, a craft market, a cinema complex and a microbrewery. It is also the site of the Nelson Mandela Gateway, the departure point for all ferry tours to Robben Island, while private operators run helicopter and boat trips around the harbour and along the coastline.

The V&A Waterfront is a shopper's paradise. The main mall is the **Victoria Wharf Shopping Centre**. One of the smartest shopping malls in the country, it is a magnet for locals and tourists alike. There are shops selling local fashion labels such as YDE, Sun Godd'ess, Marion & Lindie and

Evening at Victoria Wharf

Naartjie, as well as international ones such as Alfred Dunhill, Diesel and Guess. At the **Red Shed Craft Workshop** next to Victoria Wharf you can request a made-to-order item, then watch it being made. There are fabric printers, furniture makers, jewellers and ceramicists, as well as people telling fortunes, offering tattoos or selling snacks.

The old Clock Tower

Linking Victoria Wharf with Alfred Mall, **Market Square** is an open space for exhibitions and fairs in season. To one side is the **Amphitheatre**, a venue for concerts, festival events and street theatre, and a popular meeting point.

The maritime history of the Cape is detailed in full at the **Iziko Maritime Centre** (Mon–Sun 10am–5pm; free; www.iziko.org.za) in Union Castle House on Dock Road. Exhibits include the SAS *Somerset*, the only surviving boom defence vessel in the world (visitors are free to explore the entire ship), and a number of superb models, including a splendid depiction of Cape Town Harbour as it appeared in 1886.

Other attractions reflecting the area's maritime past include the **Time Ball Tower**, once used by navigators in the bay to set their clocks, and the pedestrian swing-bridge that leads over to the old **Clock Tower**. Built as the Port Captain's office in 1883, the tower overlooks Victoria Basin and marks the original entrance to the docks. With its pointed windows and little pinnacled belfry, it has a distinctly Gothic look.

The V&A Waterfront is still an active harbour, and fishing boats, yachts and cruise liners are all to be seen there. Take to the water yourself on a charter vessel and look for the Cape fur seals enjoying the waves or sunning themselves on the docks by the Clock Tower. A host of other boat tours, and sailing, fishing and diving excursions can be taken from the V&A Waterfront.

The **Two Oceans Aquarium** (daily 9.30am–6pm; feeding times: sharks 3pm, penguins 11.30am and 2.30pm, seals 11am and 2pm; charge; tel: 021-418 3823; www.aquarium.co.za) showcases the unique ecosystem of the Cape Peninsula, with its extraordinary bounty of fish, birds, mammals, reptiles and plant life from the Indian and Atlantic oceans. Stunning exhibits include a five-storey, glass-enclosed kelp forest, and a vast, mesmerising tank containing sharks, turtles and numerous large predators. There are also seal and penguin pools. Touch pools allow visitors to examine some of the friendlier creatures at first hand. This is a great favourite with children and adults alike. Qualified scuba-divers can swim amongst the ragged-tooth sharks in the Predator Exhibit or dive in the Kelp Forest.

Children also enjoy **Scratch Patch** (daily 9am–5.30pm; free, but you are required to spend a minimum of R10; www.scratchpatch.co.za). The inspiration behind this place is the amazing variety of minerals in South Africa. You can have fun picking out your favourite stones from the colourful heaps scattered about, have them weighed, then take them home and keep them in deep bowls on the coffee table.

Sea Mountain

The local Khoikhoi name for Table Mountain, Hoerikwaggo (Mountain in the Sea) has been revived by SANParks as the name of a six-day hiking trail, currently under construction, connecting Table Mountain to Cape Point.

The view past the V&A Waterfront towards Table Mountain

TABLE MOUNTAIN

Standing 1,086m (3,500ft plus) tall and measuring nearly 3km (2 miles) across, **Table Mountain** was declared a National Monument in 1957 and more recently became the centrepiece of an eponymous national park covering most uninhabited parts of the Cape Peninsula. The mountain is also part of the Cape Floral Kingdom Unesco World Heritage Site.

No visit to Cape Town is complete without taking in the unforgettable bird's-eye views from the summit. All facets of city life are spread out below in miniature – a myriad of ships in the bay, fine houses in wealthy suburbs, beautiful beaches, historic buildings, soaring skyscrapers and grim shanty towns.

The weather at the top of the mountain can change very quickly. One moment it is in sparkling sunshine, the next, shrouded in cloud – the 'Tablecloth' that sits on top and spills

On top of Table Mountain

down over the edges. If you want to go up the mountain, the golden rule is that if you can see the top, go now!

The brief but exhilarating cable-car ride to the top of Table Mountain is, in itself, an adventure to be treasured. The original **Cableway** was opened in 1929 and proved immediately popular. Over 800,000 visitors a year choose to travel to the summit in this way, and to meet this demand, the latest technology was imported from Switzerland in 1997. The cable cars revolve 360° in the course of the journey, ensuring that all passengers enjoy every part of the panorama. Letters bearing the Table Mountain postmark can be sent from the souvenir shop at the summit, and there are plenty of viewing platforms and a self-service restaurant.

The Cableway operates daily, weather permitting, departing from the Lower Cable Station every few minutes. In peak season, book tickets in advance from Lower Cable Station or the V&A Waterfront Visitors Centre to avoid a lengthy queue.

The indigenous flora and fauna to be found here are truly memorable. Table Mountain is home to almost 1,500 species of plants, some found nowhere else in the world, and the renowned Kirstenbosch National Botanical Gardens run down from its eastern flank. Whatever the season, you are sure to see stunning flowers, such as wild orchids with their glorious range of colours, and other magnificent vegetation including the spectacular Silver Tree. Wildlife is also plentiful, including porcupines, dassies (or rock hyraxes), grysbok (a small, nocturnal antelope) and baboons.

There are over 300 footpaths on the mountain, ranging from the undemanding to those best tackled only by experts, and it is a sensible precaution to contact the Mountain Club of South Africa (Mon–Fri 10am–2pm; tel: 021-465 3412) or a reputable local tour operator if you are planning a lengthy hike. In the early morning the mountain slopes are in shade, making climbing a much cooler experience.

Table Mountain is flanked by smaller mountains. To the right, when viewed from the city, are **Lion's Head** and **Signal Hill**, and to the left, **Devil's Peak**. The west face of Table Mountain comprises a series of distinctive rock formations called the **Twelve Apostles**. On a clear day you can see the entire city, V&A Waterfront and Table Bay to the north, Camps Bay and the Twelve Apostles to the west, the mountains of Stellenbosch and the Cape Flats townships to the east, and sometimes even Cape Point to the south, all from within 100m (325ft) of the cable-car station. A walk along the plateau gives views of the Southern Suburbs down to False Bay in the south.

The views of the city and Table Mountain from Signal Hill Road, which links Lion's Head to Signal Hill, are also outstanding. Signal Hill was originally a signalling post for communication with ships out at sea, and the Noon Gun is still fired from here each day. For a romantic view of the lights of Cape Town set against a floodlit Table Mountain, drive up Signal Hill at night.

The oddball dassie

The most characteristic mammal on Table Mountain is the peculiar dassie (rock hyrax), which looks like an overgrown rodent but is a relic of a once prolific ungulate family whose closest living relatives are elephants.

SOUTHERN SUBURBS

The lush suburbs south of Cape Town are an increasingly popular base from which to explore the city. Extending east from the slopes of Table Mountain and south towards the False Bay coast, they have excellent hotels and guest houses in safe neighbourhoods, and great shopping, restaurants and entertainment. From their comfortable streets, rich in fine Cape Dutch and Victorian houses, it is easy to get to vineyards, forests and gardens of tremendous beauty, yet they are just 15–20 minutes' drive from the heart of the city.

Kirstenbosch National Botanical Gardens

The fabulous **Kirstenbosch National Botanical Gardens** (daily Apr–Aug 8am–6pm, Sept–Mar 8am–7pm; charge; tel: 021-799 8783; www.sanbi.org), south of the suburb of Newlands, contains one of the world's most important botanical collections. It was founded in 1913 by Professor Henry Pearson, on the huge garden site bequeathed to the nation by Cecil Rhodes. Few places on the planet are as rich in floral variety as the Western Cape, and these magnificent gardens contain almost 7,000 species of native wild plants set in an awe-inspiring location under the watchful eye of Table Mountain.

Jurassic plants

Shaped like squatted palm trees, cycads do not merely look prehistoric, but are the last living representatives of the earliest flowering plants. It is thought that their spiky leaves evolved in the Jurassic Period as protection against herbivorous dinosaurs.

You can easily spend a full day here, following the numerous walking trails. They lead you through densely planted areas alive with scent and colour, up the rocky slopes of Table Mountain to the edge of tree-lined ravines. Other highlights include herb and fragrance gardens, pink-flowering protea shrubs

(South Africa's national plant) and prehistoric cycads.

The Gardens are very definitely a must-see item for visitors to Cape Town. Even a few hours spent in their leafy confines will give you an idea of the incredible wealth of flora in this area. There is a restaurant and a charming café, and a nursery selling seeds, plants and books. On Sunday evenings during the summer months, open-air concerts, ranging from jazz to classical to rock, are held here. For a lasting memory, enjoy a leisurely picnic and a bottle of crisp white wine in this beautiful setting.

Kirstenbosch National
Botanical Gardens

Many of the paths are hilly and the sun can be very hot, so take your time. There is ample shade, though, and a gentle breeze much of the time. The signage isn't very good, so it is wise to equip yourself with a map before you wander into this botanical heaven. If you have difficulty walking, cart tours are available, and there is a special Braille tour for the blind.

On the last Sunday of each month (except June–August) the Kirstenbosch Craft Market is held here. The quality of the goods on sale is strictly controlled by the Botanical Society, which insists that they must be crafted by hand and that the maker of the goods be present at the market. In addition to clothing, ceramics, beadwork and sculptures, there are also some very good food stalls.

Groot Constantia Estate

Constantia

Constantia is another of the great attractions in the Southern Suburbs. Nestled into the lower slopes of Table Mountain and the Constantiaberg Mountains, and enjoying views of False Bay, Constantia was the birthplace of the wine industry in South Africa.

This luscious spot was chosen by the Governor of Cape Town, Simon Van der Stel, for his own estate, out of the vast expanse of rich farmland he was given by the Dutch East India Company. Where the governor led, other high-ranking families followed, and consequently Constantia is rich in beautiful old Cape Dutch architecture. Van der Stel planted the first vines on his estate in 1685.

After Van der Stel's death, his estate was divided into three smaller estates and sold. The largest estate, **Groot Constantia** (daily 10am–5pm; free; www.grootconstantia. co.za), is still an active winery, with the added attraction that it contains the original manor house, which is now a museum. The house was founded by Van der Stel but took its modern shape around 1790–1803 under its then owner, Hendrik Cloete, who also commissioned the Anton Anreith sculpture in the niche. Although badly damaged by fire in 1925, it has been meticulously restored to its original state, and is quite beautiful. Wine-tastings and tours of the modern cellars are available, and there is a good restaurant in the old stables.

The other estates in the Constantia Winelands are **Steenberg** (www.steenberg-vineyards.co.za), **Klein Constantia** (www.kleinconstantia.com), **Constantia Uitsig** (www.constantia-uitsig.com) and **Buitenverwachting** (literally, 'Beyond Expectation'; www.buitenverwachting.co.za).

They are all arguably a little less formal than Groot Constantia, but just as pretty, and all have excellent restaurants and offer wine-tasting sessions, typically from around 9am–4pm Monday to Friday and 9am–noon on Saturday. The produce of all these vineyards is amongst the best the Cape has to offer, but the ultimate souvenir has to be Klein Constantia's Vin de Constance, a modern re-creation of the fine dessert wine so beloved by Napoleon, sold in a replica of the original bottle.

Carpets of Flowers

Though the smallest of the world's six floral kingdoms, the Cape Floral Kingdom is the richest, boasting an incredible 8,600 species of wild plants, 5,800 of which are found nowhere else on earth.

The most common vegetation is *fynbos* ('fine bush'). This comprises three families: proteas, which come in all shapes and sizes, all deeply coloured; restios, the hardy ground-cover used for thatching; and the delicate ericas, similar to heathers.

The Cape comes alive with spring flowers in September and October, with the most spectacular displays drawing massive crowds. Huge traffic jams build up along routes through vast regions carpeted with brightly coloured blooms as far as the eye can see. Many towns and villages hold wild-flower festivals at this time of year to celebrate the natural wonder on their doorstep.

Irma Stern Museum

Other Suburbs

South Africa's most famous artist, Irma Stern (1894–1966), once lived at The Firs (Cecil Road, Rosebank), and this small house is now the excellent **Irma Stern Museum** (Tue–Sat 10am–5pm; charge; www.irmastern.co.za). A fantastically versatile and prolific painter, Stern's main claim to fame was that she introduced the European Expressionist concept to African art. The collection includes an absorbing and representative collection of Stern's own work, but also a collection of finely crafted Africana collected during her extensive travels around the continent. The fine **Baxter Theatre Complex**, one of the most important centres for the arts in Cape Town, is also in Rosebank.

Rondebosch, south of Rosebank, is distinguished by a number of particularly elegant 19th-century buildings, including the rather grand **University of Cape Town**. Cecil Rhodes built a great estate, Groote Schuur, which is now the official home of the President of South Africa. The legacy of the 19th-century prime minister can be seen in many of the street names throughout the area. On the slopes of Devil's Peak, off Rhodes Drive, stone steps and majestic sculpted lions lead to the **Rhodes Memorial** (www.rhodesmemorial.co.za), which is styled after a Greek temple, but with a nod to Nelson's Column. You can enjoy tremendous views over the Cape Flats to the Hottentots Holland and Helderberg Mountains from the adjoining coffee shop. Visible below the

Memorial is the thatched **Mostert's Mill**, built here in 1796 when the surrounding land was wheat fields.

Sports fans are drawn to the suburb of Newlands by the **Newlands Cricket and Rugby Stadia**, homes to the Western Cape's provincial cricket and rugby unions, which regularly host domestic and international cricket and rugby matches. Newlands is also home to the **South African Rugby Museum** on Boundary Road, the largest rugby museum in the world. Exhibits date back to 1891, and it is a veritable shrine to the national Springbok team that won the Rugby World Cup in 1995 and 2007. A working watermill, the **Josephine Mill**, is also on Boundary Road. Although it is now the office of the Cape Town Historical Society, the mill still produces flour, and visitors can buy the flour and products made from it. The charming tea garden is the venue for concerts during the summer.

The Grecian Rhodes Memorial

Shoppers head for plush Cavendish Square in Claremont, while horse-racing fans flock to nearby Kenilworth.

Wynberg is the site of the **Maynardville Open-Air Theatre**, which puts on Shakespeare plays on summer evenings (these typically run from 10 Jan–20 Feb; tel: 021-421 7695; www.maynardville.co.za).

A drive through the suburbs makes you all too well aware of the great divide between rich and poor that still exists

Township Tours

The townships that cover the sandy flats east of Cape Town were created under apartheid, when tens of thousands of 'non-white' Capetonians were forcibly evicted from more central suburbs such as District Six after they were re-zoned as 'whites only'. The Cape Flats thus became a hotbed of anti-apartheid feeling, as well as poverty-related crime, and while the area has experienced significant improvement since 1994, it is still unwise to explore unguided.

As a result, 'township tours' led by local residents are now offered by most Cape Town operators, a highly rewarding experience that often starts with a visit to the District Six Museum before heading out to a township. One of the most regularly visited, the shanty town of **Khayelitsha** – Xhosa for 'Our New Home' – was created in the 1950s and now supports some 500,000 people. Cape Town's oldest 'black' township is **Langa**, which was founded in 1927 a few kilometres east of the city centre, and has a more established feel about it than Khayelitsha.

The small township of **Imizamo Yethu** – Xhosa for 'Through Collective Struggle' – was established outside Hout Bay in the dying years of apartheid. A study in contrasts, this encampment of 15,000 residents has an incredibly picturesque setting, yet living conditions are harsh and amenities minimal. For all that, the atmosphere is welcoming, and informative two-hour tours run by local residents leave daily at 10.30am, 1pm and 4pm – tel: 083-719 4870 for details.

here. To the east lie the bleak expanses of the **Cape Flats** townships, where Africans and Coloureds inhabit their own separate areas in a painful legacy of South Africa's recent past. Life here is still harsh, all too frequently violent, and conditions squalid, yet visitors are often surprised and heartened by the positive attitude and courage of many of the inhabitants. Tourists wishing to explore the Cape Flats are firmly advised not

Township kids

to travel here alone. The only safe way is via one of the township tours *(see box opposite and page 118).*

ROBBEN ISLAND

Lying 10km (6 miles) off the north coast of Cape Town, **Robben Island** is a vivid and poignant reminder of South Africa's troubled political past, for it was here that opponents of apartheid – most famously, Nelson Mandela and Walter Sisulu – were held. An integral part of the country's history and an essential item on any itinerary around Cape Town, it is now a national museum and wildlife reserve, and was made a Unesco World Heritage Site in 1999.

Mandela spent 19 years in the place he once described as 'the harshest, most iron-fisted outpost in the South African penal system', and the tiny cell which was his 'home' for nearly two decades has become a shrine for the tens of thousands of tourists who visit each year. Once you have seen it,

In the prison

you can only marvel at this remarkable man, and realise what an incredible moment it was when he returned to that cell during the Millennium celebration to light a candle to mark hope for the future.

Robben Island may only be visited on the official guided tours that depart hourly from the Nelson Mandela Gateway on V&A Waterfront from 9am–3pm and take 3½ hours, inclusive of the return ferry trip (charge; tel: 021-419 1300; www.robben-island.org.za). Many other operators offer 'trips to Robben Island', but these only view the island from the boat and do not actually land passengers.

Visitors can see the cells where dozens of inmates endured appalling conditions, the lime quarry where prisoners damaged their eyesight working in the unremitting glare, and the house where Robert Sobukwe served years of solitary confinement. The leper graveyard and church are a reminder of the other outcasts who shared this man-made hell.

By the time Nelson Mandela arrived on Robben Island in 1964 this tiny island had been infamous for its brutality for over three centuries. It housed political opponents of whatever regime was in power, criminals, the insane and lepers alike.

Dutch settlers, who named the island after the *robbe* (seals) that once bred there, first used it as prison in the 1660s. The earliest political prisoner was a Khoikhoi leader called Autshumato. A succession of political detainees followed, including Muslim holy men. The mosque close to the prison is a shrine to these men, who were the founders of Islam on the Cape.

From the mid-1800s the island was increasingly used as a hospital. This diversification didn't lessen the brutality. Patients lived in terrible conditions, with the chronically sick afforded no more consideration than criminals or political dissidents.

In spite of its notorious past, Robben Island is seen as a positive symbol. Ahmed Kathrada, head of the Ex-Political Prisoners Committee, who spent almost 20 years there, said: 'We want it to reflect the triumph of freedom and human dignity over oppression and humiliation, of courage and determination over weakness, of a new South Africa over the old.'

Robert Sobukwe House

Visiting the island is a moving and remarkable experience. The tour guides, ex-inmates, provide a graphic insight into life, or rather existence, inside the prison. At times it is a harrowing exerience, yet the guides communicate with humour and a positive attitude that is both humbling and uplifting. Ex-warders now work alongside those who were once interred here. In A-Wing the prison security intercom system has been ingeniously adapted to relate 'Cell Stories'. You can activate these to hear the voices of former prisoners describing their experiences.

An often neglected aspect of Robben Island is its wildlife, which includes introduced antelope, the country's third-largest breeding colony of African penguins, and 74 other bird species. In the spring the place is alive with colourful flowers, while the waters offshore teem with abalone (a type of large marine snail) and crayfish. Dolphins and seals are often seen on the boat trip from the mainland.

As the boat leaves at the end of the tour, you may have mixed emotions, but you cannot help feeling a deep admiration for all those who suffered here. That this former purgatory has been transformed into such a remarkable experience is testimony to the spirit of all who lived under the malignant apartheid regime.

EXCURSIONS

Another joy of Cape Town is the variety of tempting destinations close by, including the world-famous Garden Route and the Winelands. Whether you have just a day to spare, or the luxury of taking some longer breaks around the Western Cape, you'll be spoilt for choice.

Cape Peninsula to Cape Point

A drive to the Cape of Good Hope, returning to Cape Town via the False Bay coast, makes a superb full-day excursion, incorporating glorious beaches, colourful fishing ports, stunning views of mountains and ocean, and a multitude of indigenous flora and fauna.

The colourful beach huts on the east coast of the peninsula

West Coast

Head southwest out of the city centre along the coastal road, past striped **Mouille Point Lighthouse**, the oldest in South Africa, and **Clifton**, an area known as 'Millionaires' Row,' with some of the country's most expensive homes. After the family resort of Camps Bay, the shoreline opens up, giving great views, and the road runs along the foot of the Twelve Apostles. The shoreline is popular with divers, and shipwrecks are visible from the road. Further along, **Llandudno** is a small, elite village in an outstanding setting with a gorgeous beach.

Continue on Victoria Road to the fishing town of **Hout Bay**. Take time to wander around Mariner's Wharf complex, with its fish market and seafood restaurants. You can take a boat trip to see the seals and seabirds on Duiker Island, visit the Hout Bay Museum on Andrews Road (Tue–Fri 9am–5pm; charge), or check out the World of Birds (daily 9am–5pm; charge; www.worldofbirds.org.za).

Chapman's Peak Drive, one of the most scenic routes in the Western Cape, winds along 10km (6 miles) from Hout Bay to Noordhoek. The road took seven years to carve out of the mountain face and first opened in 1922. Now a toll road, it rises to 600m (almost 2,000ft) above the ocean, with several narrow parking spots where you can pull over and admire breathtaking views down a sheer drop to the water below.

Noordhoek is home to many artists, and from October to May it is possible to visit some of their studios along the Noordhoek Art Route. The nearby hamlet of **Kommetjie**, at the end of a tidal lagoon, is hugely popular for watersports. Surfing competitions are often held at Long Beach, on which lies the wreck of a steamer that foundered during a storm in 1900.

A detour along the M65 out of Kommetjie leads to **Masiphumelele**, a Xhosa township founded in the mid-1980s, when its residents were subjected to repeated forcible removals to Khayelitsha on the Cape Flats. Initially known by the prosaic name of Site Five, Masiphumelele means 'We Will Succeed', and it now houses almost 30,000 people, most of them Xhosas from the defunct 'homeland' of Ciskei.

Baboons are a common sight in the Table Mountain National Park

Nature Reserve

Now part of the Table Mountain National Park, the **Cape of Good Hope Nature Reserve** (daily Oct–Mar 6am–6pm, Apr–Sept 7am–5pm; charge; www.tmnp.co.za) protects 8,094 hectares (20,000 acres) of stunningly beautiful windswept crags and fynbos-clad slopes. It is home to over 1,000 species of indigenous flora, and in the

The dizzying cliffs at Cape Point

spring hardy wild flowers brave gale-force winds to provide a brilliant show of colour. Wildlife includes the Cape mountain zebra, bontebok, eland and ostriches. Although the baboon population can look entertaining, repeated – and strictly forbidden – feeding by tourists has made them aggressive. You can explore the reserve by car or on foot, but take care when hiking, as the vegetation is home to cobras and puff-adders.

At **Cape Point** a funicular railway runs from the visitors centre to the **Cape Point Lighthouse**. There are spectacular views of the **Cape of Good Hope** and along the Cape. The water smashes against the rocks a dizzying distance below. The old lighthouse was superseded in 1914 by a more powerful one, after a Portuguese liner was wrecked. Marine life includes whales, dolphins and seals. There is a fine restaurant with fantastic views across to Muizenberg and the False Bay coastline. There are also plenty of picnic and barbecue spots, and great walking along miles of unspoilt beaches.

East Coast

Immediately outside the entrance to the Reserve, the private **Cape Point Ostrich Farm** (hourly tours daily 9.30am– 4.30pm; charge; www.capepointostrichfarm.com) offers a fun opportunity to meet and learn about the world's largest bird at close quarters. It is a popular activity with children, while eager souvenir-hunters can pick up all manner of ostrich-derived goods, from hollowed-out giant eggs to plush leatherware, and the ostrich platter makes for a great low-fat lunch.

On leaving the Reserve, head up the coast road towards **Simon's Town**. The home of the **South African Naval Museum**, it was once a major naval base and still has close links with the service. Look out for the statue in Jubilee Square that pays tribute to a Great Dane dog called Just Nuisance, the mascot of British sailors based here during World War II.

Simon's Town's greatest attraction lies just south of the town, at **Boulders Beach** (daily 8am–5pm, 6.30am–7.30pm in summer; charge; www.tmnp.co.za), which now forms part of Table Mountain National Park. Boulders and the adjacent Foxy Beach support a colony of around 3,000 black-and-white **African penguins**, and these delightful, charismatic creatures can be observed swimming, squabbling and waddling around the beach from a series of raised wooden walkways. Although the two main beaches and walkways lie within the national park, the connecting Willis Walk is open free of charge 24 hours a day, and it usually offers good views of penguins and other marine birds.

Fish Hoek is one of the best whale-watching spots along the Cape Peninsula. From **Jager's Walk**, a concrete walkway which runs towards Simon's Town, it is possible to get incredible views of these magnificent mammals from July to November. In 1927 ancient burial sites were discovered at Fish Hoek, in Peers Cave, the walls of which are covered in ancient paintings.

If you have time, head off-route along Kommetjie Road to **Silvermine Nature Reserve** (daily 8am–6pm; charge; www.sanparks.co.za), whose fynbos-draped slopes are home to a great diversity of mammals and birds, as well as some spectacular winter-blooming king proteas. Recently incorporated into Table Mountain National Park, the reserve runs parallel to Kalk Bay, a lively fishing port, where you can buy fish straight off the brightly painted boats.

Continuing east from Fish Hoek you come to **Muizenberg**. In the 1920s Muizenberg was the haunt of the rich and famous, many of whom built holiday homes here. The diverse architectural styles are fascinating, with fine Edwardian houses contrasting with fishermen's cottages, and colourful bathing huts line the beaches. Muizenberg Pavilion is popular with children, who enjoy the waterslide and camel rides. It is also the site of a Sunday morning flea market.

Braying birds

The African penguin was until recently known as the jackass penguin, in reference to the comic braying call that welcomes visitors to Boulders Beach.

In truth, Muizenberg is now rather seedy, but it still has plenty of interest. Many of the personal belongings of Cecil Rhodes can be seen at **Rhodes Cottage**. This simple, thatched building, once Rhodes's holiday home, is now a museum.

Stellenbosch and the Winelands

Within 30 minutes' drive of Cape Town along the N1 lie over 100 vineyards, where wine-tasting can be enjoyed in delightful surroundings. A tour of this scenic region is also a visual delight. White, gabled Cape Dutch houses and farm buildings are set against the bright green of vines in full leaf, and dwarfed by towering mountains. Fine restaurants, antique markets and gourmet food shops abound, whilst museums give a glimpse of rural colonial life.

An elegant Cape Dutch house

South Africa has a long history of wine production. Jan Van Riebeeck planted the first vines in the country, but things really developed after Huguenot refugees arrived from France in the late 17th century, bringing their winemaking expertise with them. The Western Cape is the key region, producing thousands of individual wines from many hundreds of vineyards. All types of wine are made here, but the country is best-known for its fabulous whites, and for Pinotage, a fruity, almost purple wine made from a unique cross between Pinot Noir and Cinsaut grapes, first developed in Stellenbosch.

The Stellenbosch Wine Route is the oldest and most famous of several established in recent years throughout the Winelands, each incorporating vineyards of varying sizes. All vineyards offer wine-tasting, usually from 10am–4pm on weekdays and over more restricted hours on Saturday and Sunday, and many have restaurants and shops. Following two or three routes, exploring their towns and attractions, can easily take the better part of a week. It is possible to experience many of the pleasures of the Winelands in a day, but taking two days with an overnight stop can make for a more relaxing excursion. It is best to visit in summer, when the vines are in leaf, or at harvest time when they display their autumn foliage and there's plenty of activity.

Accommodation in this area is excellent, with many fine small country hotels and guest houses, often in beautiful old buildings, including the oldest country inn in South Africa, **D'Ouwe Werf** in Stellenbosch. Additionally, some vineyards offer overnight accommodation.

Cape Dutch Architecture

Unique to South Africa, the Cape Dutch architectural style is essentially an 18th-century adaptation of a classical European building style to African conditions. The genre's distinguishing characteristic, common in older houses all around the Western Cape, though less so in Cape Town than in small towns and rural areas, is an ornate round gable standing tall above the front entrance, a feature derived from medieval houses in Amsterdam. Typical Cape Dutch houses have a steeply pitched thatched roof and whitewashed walls. The oldest houses were built to a U- or T-shaped floor plan, while more ostentatious examples built after the mid-18th century have an H-shaped floor plan.

The classic contours of the Cape Dutch style are especially well complemented by the shady glades and neat vineyards of the Cape Winelands, which is where the finest examples are found. Particularly worthwhile are the manor houses of the Vergelegen, Libertas, Boschendal and Groot Constantia Wine Estates, the Old Dutch Reformed church in Franschhoek, and any number of old townhouses lining Stellenbosch's Dorp Street.

On the Stellenbosch Wine Route

Stellenbosch

First settled in 1679, **Stellenbosch** is the second-oldest town in South Africa. It is now a busy university town, and no longer a pretty Winelands village, though the historic quarter retains its architectural charm. The town was nicknamed Eikestad (Oaktown) due to the old oaks that line its streets. There are plenty of good shops in the town, and some lovely Cape Dutch, Georgian and Victorian houses.

The best starting point for a leisurely tour is the oak-shaded village green known as **De Braak**. The green is surrounded by old buildings, notably a Powder House built in 1777, the Anglican Church of St Mary (1852) and the Rhenish Church (1823). A block further south, **Dorp Street** is lined by a series of marvellously ornate Cape Dutch facades, most of which date to the 19th century or earlier. These include a fascinating shop which has changed little over the past century: **Oom Samie Se Winkel** ('Uncle Samie's Store') is packed with handmade crafts, wines, basketry, dried fruit, antiques, lacework and farm implements, and tea is served in the restaurant.

The **Village Museum** (Mon–Sat 9.30am–5pm, Sun 2–5pm; charge; www.museums.org.za/stellmus) on Ryneveld Street is a complex of historic houses, depicting in remarkable detail the life of the townsfolk over three centuries – even the gardens are perfectly in period. Directly opposite, the imposing neo-Gothic **Moederkerk** was built on the site of the original Dutch Reformed church, which burnt down in 1710. The **Stellenryck Wine Museum** in Strand Street covers the history of winemaking, while the fascinating **Toy and Miniature Museum** is in an old rectory at the corner of Market and Herte Streets, next to the Tourist Office.

For art-lovers, the **Sasol Art Museum** (Mon–Fri 9am–5pm, Sat 9am–1pm; charge) is home to the University of Stellenbosch's excellent collection, and it also has displays of prehistoric artefacts. A more recent addition is the **Rupert Gallery** (Mon–Fri 9am–4pm, Sat 9am–noon; charge), which lies on Lower Dorp Street overlooking the Eerste River, and displays 350 contemporary South African artworks collected by the late Dr Anton Rupert and his wife Huberte.

The **Stellenbosch Wine Route** includes at least 100 estates. Popular estates close to Stellenbosch include **Blaauwklippen**, with its fine restaurant housed in a thatched manor house and coach museum where visitors can take rides on some of the old carts and gigs, and **Morgenhof**, at the foot of the Simonsberg Mountains, which produces outstanding wines, including Merlot and Cabernet Sauvignon, from its beautiful estate. Arguably the vineyard most geared to entertaining families is **Spier**, which boasts the famed Jonkershuis Restaurant, offers pony rides, and holds concerts at its open-air amphitheatre. A section of the estate has been given over to a conservation group that has used it to house a family of hand-reared cheetahs, and visitors can stroke these beautiful spotted creatures. One of the smallest and oldest wineries, **Kanonkop**, has an exceptional range of award-winning wines, renowned worldwide.

The R310 northeast from Stellenbosch towards Franschhoek takes you through the stunning Helshoogte Pass, and some of the most beautiful scenery in the Winelands. Head up to the 'vineyard in the sky', **Delaire**. From here, the view of the Simonsberg Mountains and across the Franschhoek Valley is memorable, particularly at sunset. **Boschendal**, an estate on the other side of the Pass, just before the junction with the R45, combines the opportunity to sample excellent red wines with a tour of a magnificent Cape Dutch manor, furnished in spectacular 17th- and 18th-century style.

Franschhoek

Franschhoek, set in a valley with mountains on three sides, is the culinary showpiece of the Western Cape. With some 30 restaurants offering outstanding Cape Malay and Provençal cuisine, it has become a popular place for fashionable Capetonians to wine and dine.

This pretty village was founded in 1680 by Huguenots who came over from France. Their story is told in detail at the **Huguenot Memorial Museum** (Mon–Sat 9am–5pm, Sun 2–5pm; charge; www.museum.co.za), which lies on Lambrecht Street alongside the **Huguenot Monument**, paying tribute to these French settlers.

A number of vineyards can be reached on foot from here, with the majority lying off Huguenot and Main roads. At **Cabrière Estate**, off the Franschhoek Pass, renowned winemaker Achim von Arnim demonstrates the art of *sabrage*, slicing the neck of a bottle of sparkling wine with a sabre. The cellar at **Mont Rochelle** is decorated with stained-glass and chandeliers, and there is a stud farm at **Chamonix**.

Huguenot Monument, Franschhoek

Paarl

The R303 leads northwest from Franschhoek to **Paarl**, the largest Winelands town, home to the **KWV**, the giant wine-growing co-operative. The KWV's 22-hectare (54-acre) cellar complex here is the largest in the world, featuring the awe-inspiring Cathedral Cellar, with a barrel-vaulted roof.

Paarl is rather industrialised and has lost its charm, but has two main claims to historical significance. Here, in 1875, the Afrikaans language was first officially recognised, a fact commemorated by the **Taal Monument** on the hill above the town, and by the **Afrikaans Taal Museum** on Pastorie Street. It is also the closest town to **Victor Verster Prison**, where Nelson Mandela spent the final years of his 27-year incarceration.

Vineyards near Paarl include **Fairview**, with its herd of Saanen goats which live in a tall stone tower. The balcony of the tasting room at **Laborie** looks across the vineyards to Paarl Mountain, and there is a beautiful rose garden.

Situated a short distance off the R101, the 7½-hectare (18½-acre) **Drakenstein Lion Park** (daily 9.30am–5pm; charge; www.lionrescue.org.za) is home to 15 lions that were born in captivity and cannot be introduced to the wild. Nearby, **Butterfly World** (daily 9am–5pm; charge) is South Africa's largest butterfly park, with more than 20 indigenous species in an attractive landscaped indoor garden, as well as a mesmerising selection of creepy spiders.

Hermanus and the Tip of Africa

The best land-based whale-watching in the world is to be found around **Hermanus**, a couple of hours' drive south-east of Cape Town. A day trip to this seaside resort can be immensely rewarding, with cliff viewpoints as little as 30m (98ft) away from these spectacular mammals. The excitement is almost tangible; reports of sightings draw crowds to the shore to watch in wonder. Hermanus can become very crowded, but there are plenty of excellent viewing spots from Betty's Bay in the west to the coast off the De Hoop Nature Reserve. When it is not whale season, this region is still well worth visiting, as it combines many of the best aspects of the Western Cape in one relatively compact area. If you have more than a day to spare, a tour of this memorable stretch of coastline can be combined with the Garden Route.

Hermanus lies 110km (68 miles) from Cape Town on the shores of Walker Bay. The quickest route from the city is via the N2, over Sir Lowry's Pass, with its stunning views down to False Bay, then via the R43.

The **Vergelegen Wine Estate** (daily 9am–4.30pm; charge; www.vergelegen.co.za), near Somerset West, is widely regarded as the most beautiful wine farm in South Africa. Situated on the slopes of the Helderberg Mountains, Vergelegen, which means 'lying afar', started life as a remote outpost of the Cape Colony in 1685 and was later bought by Willem van der Stel, who founded the historic manor house. The magnificent gardens and architecture are complemented by the opportunity to taste its selection of award-winning wines.

An alternative route to Hermanus is via the R44, which forks off the N2 at Somerset West, then follows the coast around. At Betty's Bay, the renowned **Harold Porter National Botanical Garden** (daily 8am–4.30pm; charge; www.sanbi.org) has more than 1,600 species of fynbos. The wildlife here is elusive, but includes baboons and leopards. Nearby **Stoney Point** rivals Hermanus for whale-watching, and is home to a colony of African penguins.

The R320, which forks off the R43 2km (1 mile) before Hermanus (the sign reads 'to Caledon'), leads to three **vineyards**, Whale Haven, Hamilton Russell and Bouchard Finlayson. The Walker Bay wines produced by these estates are among the most respected and expensive in the country.

Walker Bay is one of the world's top whale watching sites

Originally a fishing and whaling village, Hermanus is now a popular resort, but the whales continue to contribute to the town's finances – through tourism. The **Old Harbour Museum** (Mon–Sat 9am–4.30pm; charge; www.hermanus.co.za) tells the story of the whaling industry, and the mysterious and soothing songs of the whales out at sea are caught by sonar buoy and transmitted live into the museum.

Hermanus is home to the world's only **Whale Crier**, who strides through the streets, announcing whale sightings on his unique kelp horn. A toll-free Whale Hotline (tel: 028-312 2629) also keeps would-be watchers updated.

East of Hermanus is Bredasdorp, home to some fine Cape Dutch buildings, as well as the popular **Shipwreck Museum** (Mon–Fri 9am–4.30pm, Sat–Sun 11am–4pm; charge), with relics recovered from the region's notorious waters.

Gentle Giants

From June to December, the waters around the Western Cape host some rare visitors – migrating whales which breed and calve in sheltered bays along the coastline.

For several months whale calves can be seen swimming and playing with their mothers. This joyous display is truly unforgettable. Peak viewing time is August to November, and many towns along the route hold annual Whale Festivals to welcome these gentle giants.

Humpback and Bryde's whales can be spotted, but the most common sightings are of southern right whales. With tragic irony, the ages-old, instinctive breeding journey of these magnificent mammals nearly brought about their extinction. Southern right whales were so named because they were the 'right' quarry for whalers. Every bit of these slow-moving mammals could be used, and conveniently, they floated when dead, making retrieval of the bodies easy. Over 12,000 were killed in these waters. Now protected, the population is increasing at a rate of 7 percent per year.

The Tip of Africa

Forty-five km (28 miles) south of Bredastorp, **Cape Agulhas** is the southernmost point of Africa. It is here, and not at the Cape of Good Hope, as is often thought, that the Indian and Atlantic oceans meet. This spot is marked by a cairn a short distance from **Agulhas Lighthouse**. Unlike the Cape of Good Hope with its dramat-

Humpback whale

ic cliffs, the coast at Agulhas slopes gently into the ocean – next stop, Antarctica. Nearby Struisbaai boasts an immaculate 14km (8-mile) beach, the longest uninterrupted stretch of white sand in Southern Africa.

East of Cape Agulhas lies the idyllic village of **Arniston**, named after a ship wrecked here in 1815. Locals call it Waenhuiskrans, after an enormous cavern eroded into the cliffs close to the village. The landscape here is simply stunning. Near the harbour, historic thatched fishermen's cottages look over a turquoise sea with rolling white sand dunes in the distance.

Protecting the largest surviving tract of coastal fynbos, the unforgettable **De Hoop Nature Reserve** (daily 7am–6pm; charge; www.capenature.co.za) lies 15km (9 miles) northeast of Arniston, but it is reached by returning to Bredasdorp, then taking a well-marked dirt road. A rich variety of wildlife is associated with the profuse fynbos, including bontebok, Cape mountain zebra, and over 250 species of birds, including a rare breeding colony of Cape vultures. The reserve has 50km (30 miles) of spectacular coastline, flanked by pristine white sand dunes rising as high as 90m (295ft). This stretch of water is the breeding ground for most of the Cape's whales.

The Garden Route

With the exception of Table Mountain, the Garden Route is the best-known tourist destination on the Western Cape. Though its name conjures up visions of an area abundant in floral splendour, many visitors are surprised to find that it is more forest than garden. The title 'Garden Route' reflects the lush vegetation covering the rolling hills lying between the dramatic Tsitsikamma Mountains and the breathtaking shoreline of the Indian Ocean, home to whales and dolphins.

The beautiful Garden Route is a popular tourist destination

This is a popular resort area for South African holidaymakers and can become very congested during their main holiday season. Increasing over-development to meet the demand of the tourists has resulted in the inevitable loss of some of the natural beauty, and to many the Garden Route will be a disappointment. However, there are still many unspoilt jewels to enjoy.

The Garden Route is often thought to stretch the 800km (497 miles) from Cape Town to Port Elizabeth, but actually begins at Mossel Bay, some 400km (248 miles) east of Cape Town, and ends at Storms River, about 190km (118 miles) further east. This is covered by the excellent N2, but truly to experience the natural wealth of the area, head off the main road and take in some of the picturesque older roads through attractive coastal towns and past exquisite lakes, lagoons and rivers.

The area has numerous signposts, so it is easy to wander off-route and then return to the N2 again. You can reach Knysna on a lengthy day trip from Cape Town, but this will not allow you time to see very much. It is advisable to allow at least two days, with an overnight stop, if you really want an enduring memory to take home with you.

Mossel Bay to Wilderness

When you see the industrial approach to **Mossel Bay**, don't be put off. The centre of the town is charming. The **Bartolomeu Dias Museum Complex** (Mon–Fri 9am–4.45pm, Sat–Sun 9am–3.45pm; charge; www.diasmuseum.co.za) is well worth a visit, so take time to wander around. In its grounds you'll find the 500-year old Post Office Tree where sailors used to leave letters for passing ships, as well as a life-size replica of Bartolomeu Dias's caravel, an ethno-botanical garden, a shell museum displaying seashells from around the world, and an aquarium housing living shellfish in their natural habitat.

The swimming from Santos Beach is among the best on the Garden Route. A cruise around Seal Island will allow you to spot comical African penguins and Cape fur seals, as well as the great white sharks which feed on them. A walk through the Dana Bay Nature Reserve leads to St Blaize Lighthouse.

The **Outeniqua Choo-Tjoe** steam train travels the scenic journey between Mossel Bay and the town of George, passing through beautiful farmland, over spectacular bridges and also running alongside the dramatic coastline. There are few more relaxing ways to view one of the most beautiful stretches of Cape coastline than from the carriages of this little engine.

Eighteen km (11 miles) on from George, the N2 bisects **Wilderness**. Lavish holiday homes now sprawl along the

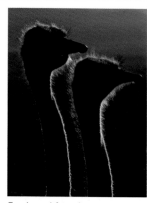

Feathered friends

dunes bordering the famed long beach of what was once a small, romantic village.

The village of Wilderness marks the start of the **Wilderness National Park** (open daily; charge; www.sanparks.org). This wetland area with its lush forests covers over 2,500 hectares (6,177 acres), stretching 28km (17½ miles) along the coastline to Sedgefield, and incorporating 15km (just over 9 miles) of inland waterways including five rivers and five lakes. It is the natural habitat for 250 species of birds, including 79 different types of waterbirds. There are a number of marked hiking trails, and it is also possible to explore the area from the water in rented canoes. In the spring, it is vibrant with multicoloured carpets of wild flowers.

Just after Sedgefield, a right turn towards Buffel's Bay leads to an unexpected gem; a glorious, undeveloped beach bordering the **Goukamma Nature Reserve** (open daily; charge; www.capenature.org.za). The beach is virtually deserted, bathers preferring the more sheltered waters of Buffel's Bay itself, just 1km (0.6 miles) further on. Goukamma covers over 200 sq km (124 square miles), including Groenvlei, a freshwater lake very popular with anglers. Rich wildlife includes fish eagles, rare African black oystercatchers, vervet monkeys, otters and mongoose. Marine life is equally plentiful; dolphins are often seen. During the breeding season (July–November), southern right whales pass by on their migration route.

Little Karoo

Just 63km (39 miles) north of Wilderness, **Oudtshoorn**, the prinicipal town of the Little Karoo, is an interesting side trip from the Garden Route. Famous for ostrich farming, the region's dry climate makes it ideal for breeding these large, flightless birds, and their favourite food grows well here. It is impossible to travel around the region without seeing flocks of them. Though once farmed for feathers, they are now farmed primarily for their low-cholesterol meat, but ostrich leather is also becoming fashionable for clothes and shoes, and their eggs are good to eat, or are painted and sold as souvenirs.

'Feather Millionaires'

Towards the end of the 19th century, the demand for ostrich plumes for the hats and feather boas of the ladies of fashion was unprecedented. Prices soared as ostrich feathers became a commodity of enormous value, and, as a consequence, many ostrich farmers around Oudtshoorn became millionaires virtually overnight.

These 'feather millionaires' threw themselves enthusiastically into the extravagant lifestyle their newfound wealth bought them. Their excesses rivalled those of the Randlords of Johannesburg, who had made countless millions from gold and diamonds.

They built themselves elaborate sandstone mansions, known as 'feather palaces,' splendid examples of which can be seen in Oudtshoorn today. Many of these were an unfortunate combination of lavish spending and questionable taste. The **Le Roux Townhouse** on High Street is a restored example of one of the greatest of these mansions. Visitors to the **Safari Ostrich Farm** on the R328 can visit Welgeluk, another 'feather palace'.

When ostrich feathers fell out of fashion at the start of World War I, the market crashed spectacularly, reducing many of the 'feather millionaires' to poverty.

Exploring the spectacular rock formations in Cango Caves

The story of this industry, which enjoyed a glorious hey-day from the 1880s until World War I, is chronicled at the excellent **C.P. Nel Museum** (Mon–Fri 8am–5pm, Sat–Sun 9am–5pm; charge) on Baron Van Rheede Street.

Many ostrich farms are open to the public. **Highgate** (off Mossel Bay Road) was the first to exploit the tourism poten-tial of ostrich farming. You can see the birds hatch, hold the chicks, watch the adults being plucked, and even go for a ride. You can also eat ostrich meat or buy ostrich-skin products.

Three km (2 miles) north of Oudtshoorn is the **Cango Wildlife Ranch** (daily 8am–4.30pm; charge; www.cango. co.za). This breeding centre for rare animals is a fantastic place to see African wildlife, including lions, crocodiles, snakes, meerkats and tortoises, as well as exotics such as jaguars and wallabies. Visitors are allowed to meet the more approachable residents, and it is an unforgettable experience to encounter playful young cheetahs.

Twenty-nine km (18 miles) further north along the R328 are the spectacular **Cango Caves** (daily 9am–4pm; charge; www.cangocaves.co.za). In 1780 a local farmer discovered this sequence of vast, ancient caverns, linked by narrow passages under the Swartberg Mountains. Over the past 100,000 years, water oozing through rock and limestone has resulted in an intricate underground landscape of stalactites and dripstone formations that is simply breathtaking.

Knysna

Knysna, 102km (63 miles) east of Mossel Bay, and a five-hour drive along the N2 from Cape Town, is situated in an attractive hilly setting on the shores of the tidal Knysna Lagoon. It is one of the main tourist destinations along the Garden Route, and a convenient place to stay, though it has lost some of its charm in the scramble to cash in on tourism. There are, however, no beaches; the Heads (two steep sandstone cliffs) and a coral reef guard the sea mouth of the lagoon. A cruise to the Heads from Knysna Quay is a popular excursion, with ferry tickets available through the tourist information bureau.

The history of the town, which grew to prosperity on the timber trade that nearly destroyed its massive hardwood forests, is told at the **Knysna Museum** (Mon–Fri 9.30am–4pm, Sat 9.30am–1pm; donations accepted) on Main Street, in a building which also houses South Africa's first Angling Museum.

To experience the **Diepwalle Forest** (daily 6am–6pm; charge; www.sanparks.org) take the R339, a well-maintained unpaved road. Though a shadow of its former self, the forest is still impressive. If you're lucky, you will glimpse a brilliant red-and-green Knysna loerie amongst the huge, centuries-old stinkwood and yellowwood trees that form a thick canopy overhead. There is a marked Elephant Trail, and traffic signs warn of elephants crossing. Unfortunately the elephants are no longer here – the few remaining wild pachyderms were re-located to the Shamwari Game Reserve, 300km (186 miles) east of the town. The only way to see elephants now is at the zoo-like **Knysna Elephant Park** (daily 8.30am–4.30pm; charge; www.knysnaelephantpark.co.za), where some are so tame you can feed and hug them.

It is possible to buy finely crafted items, made from the Forest hardwoods, from the talented artists that sell their works in the street markets and craft shops along Main Street, and at the roadside stalls along the Garden Route from Knysna to Plettenberg Bay.

Knysna is lively at night, and has many good restaurants. If you're partial to oysters you will be in your element here – Knysna is home to one of the largest oyster farms in the world.

The Knysna Elephants

Elephants were first documented along the Cape Coast by Vasco da Gama during his pioneering 1497 voyage, when the Western Cape probably supported a population of around 50,000. Elephant numbers plummeted following European settlement, however, and by the 1870s the region's 400–500 survivors were confined to the depths of the impenetrable forests around Knysna. Even these secretive forest giants struggled to evade the hunter's bullet, and when they were finally accorded protection as royal game in 1908, only 20 were known to remain. The decline from here was gradual but inevitable, with just four surviving elephants left by 1983, and only one ageing mono-tusked female recorded in 1994.

However, experts remain optimistic that the most southerly wild population of African elephants may still prove to be viable, following the photographing of a 20-year-old bull in 2000, the reliable sighting of a two-tusked female two years later, and a 2007 faecal study suggesting that at least five different females still inhabit the forest depths – a tantalising prospect indeed for hikers!

Feeding time at Knysna Elephant Park

Plettenberg Bay and Tsitsikamma

Thirty km (18 miles) east lies **Plettenberg Bay**, a beautiful spot spoilt only by the hideous modern hotel built near the beach. It is a fashionable resort with safe bathing, and consequently gets very crowded in high summer. At the south of the bay, the scenic Robberg Peninsula, named after the seals that inhabit its base, is protected in the **Robberg Nature Reserve** (7am–5pm, Dec–Jan until 8pm; charge; www.robberg capenature.com). A round walk to the furthest end of the peninsula takes about four hours.

A large number of dolphins make Plettenberg Bay their home year-round. Boat trips around the bay run from the beach, and Ocean Blue Adventures (tel: 044-533 5083; www. oceanadventures.co.za) runs a particularly informative excursion. The experience of being in a small boat with dolphins playing in the waves, so close that you could touch them, is truly incredible. Between July and November there is also a good chance of seeing whales, and the Whale Hotline gives updates on their presence (tel: 0800-228 222).

The strikingly beautiful **Tsitsikamma National Park** (gates open 7am–7pm; charge; www.sanparks.org) encompasses hardwood forests, sparkling pools, coral reefs, dunes, long stretches of sandy beach with safe swimming spots, deep gorges, waterfalls and the Otter Trail, one of the most popular hikes in the country. The world's highest bungee jump is here. Those adventurous enough to leap off Bloukrans Bridge have a 216m (708ft) fall before they are snapped back up again.

At **Storms River Mouth**, the main tourist focus within Tsitsikamma, the Garden Route ends in a spectacular fashion. Cliffs covered in dense forest lead down to black rocks against which waves crash violently. You can walk along the boardwalk from the restaurant at Storms River Rest Camp, past the cave inhabited thousands of years ago by strandlopers (beachcombers), and gaze down at the surging waters of the river mouth from the Paul Sauer Suspension Bridge.

The West Coast and Cederberg

The 400km (248-mile) stretch of land north of Cape Town that forms the West Coast is an area of diverse beauty. It lacks the lushness of the Garden Route or the Winelands, but its attractions are considerable. The Atlantic Ocean bestows on this region a wild coastline, a rich harvest of seafood, huge and varied communities of seabirds, and the awe-inspiring spectacle of migrating whales. Inland, the rugged Cederberg Mountains form its eastern border, their fascinating rock formations a natural sculptor's gallery. Ancient rock paintings speak of human life here long before the arrival of the first Europeans, and a wealth of wildlife can be seen. Between mountains and ocean lie the wheat fields and vineyards of the Swartland, and wild flowers carpet this whole region in a springtime display of extraordinary vibrancy.

On a day-long excursion from Cape Town, you can travel along the R27, visiting the town of Darling and the West Coast National Park. Alternatively, you could head straight for the Cederberg Wilderness Area and view ancient rock paintings and remarkable natural rock sculptures. A two- to three-day excursion would accommodate a loop right around the region.

Just 10 minutes outside of Cape Town on the R27 is the resort of **Bloubergstrand**, with its unrivalled view of Table Mountain, seen across Table Bay. The small town of **Darling** lies further along the R27, 70km (43 miles) north of Cape Town. Its many attractions include handsome old buildings and a Butter Museum. The annual spring flower show, held annually since 1917, is a major event. Nearby Yzerfontein is renowned for the sweet-tasting crayfish caught in its waters.

The wetlands of the **West Coast National Park** (daily June–Sept 7am–6.30pm, Oct–May 6am–8pm; charge; www.

The view towards Table Mountain from Bloubergstrand

Eve's footprints

A set of fossilised footprints discovered in West Coast National Park in 1996 dates back 117,000 years, the oldest footprints of anatomically modern human beings known from anywhere in the world.

sanparks.org) attract millions of marine birds which find a safe home on its islands, away from ocean predators. Waders, pelicans, black oystercatchers and flamingos can all be seen around **Langebaan Lagoon**. At the southern tip of the park, the **Postberg Nature Reserve** is one of the closest areas to Cape Town for viewing spring wild flowers, and it also protects wildlife such as oryx and springbok, but is only open during the spring wild-flower season (7am–7pm; charge; tel: 022-772 2144 for opening times).

Further along the R27 lies St Helena Bay, where Vasco da Gama landed in 1497. A stone monument commemorates the landing, and the story is told at the **Da Gama Museum**.

Two hours north of St Helena Bay, the fishing port of **Lambert's Bay** is dominated by the huge colonies of seabirds 100m (328ft) offshore at **Bird Island** (daily 6am–6pm; charge; tel: 027-432 1000). You can walk out along a concrete breakwater to the island, where masses of noisy Cape gannets, cormorants and African penguins can be seen from a special viewing tower. Boat trips operate from Lambert's Bay to view visiting whales (July–November), and you can catch a glimpse of Cape fur seals, penguins and dolphins year-round. Schools of over 1,000 dolphins have been spotted.

Some 60km (37 miles) east along the R364 is the northern tip of the Cederberg Mountains and the **Cederberg Wilderness Area** (open daily; charge; www.capenature.org.za). Time and the elements have eroded the sandstone into a surreal landscape that stretches as far as the eye can see. The most extraordinary shapes are in the south of the reserve. They include the **Wolfberg Arch**, a 30m- (98ft-)

high natural archway of rock, and the **Maltese Cross**, a 22m- (66ft-) tall pillar.

Vegetation includes wild olives, purple-blue *ridderspoor*, the rare snow protea, and rooibos *(see page 104)*. The region is named after the Clanwilliam cedar tree, which grows against cliffs, overhanging at altitudes of more than 1000m (3,280ft) above sea level. Wildlife includes baboons, porcupine, aardvark, caracal, Cape fox, mongoose and leopard. Puff-adders and black spitting cobras inhabit the undergrowth, and Clanwilliam yellowfish swim in the Olifants River, named after the great herds of elephants that once roamed on the vast plains to the south of the mountains.

This region was a favourite hunting ground of Bushmen for thousands of years. Their **rock paintings** remain throughout the area, notably in the beautiful private wilderness area of Bushmans Kloof, where guided walks reveal what is known of their history.

Clanwilliam is a good base from which to explore this area. There is plenty of accommodation, a museum and, of course, rooibos tea.

Cape Town is about three hours' drive down the N7, past Citrusdal and the giant, golden wheat fields of Swartland. En route, look to the horizon for a long-distance view of Table Mountain.

African penguin

WHAT TO DO

SHOPPING

Arts and crafts from all over Africa can be bought in Cape Town. These vary in quality, but it is not difficult to find really beautifully made items at relatively low cost. Traditional West African carved wooden masks, made to celebrate events such as a birth or wedding, make a fascinating souvenir. Other African objects to look out for include soapstone carvings, intricate beadwork, colourful fabrics, basket work and wooden bowls.

Gold, diamonds and other gems both precious and semi-precious are readily available, sometimes at very low prices, and there are many talented jewellery designers working in the region. For a little fun, visit the gemstone scratch patch, at the V&A Waterfront, where you can search for semi-precious stones in giant containers, then buy them by weight.

Colonial antiques, including porcelain, glassware, furniture and jewellery, are also much in evidence, as are contemporary art, leather goods and ceramics. You will also see brightly painted ostrich eggs, and bags, wallets, belts and shoes made from ostrich skin.

Few travellers return home without at least one bottle of the fine wine for which the region is renowned, and tasting before you buy is all part of the fun. Many vineyards and wine shops will arrange to ship your purchase to your home.

Where to Shop

Cape Town and its suburbs are dotted with an ever increasing selection of malls where a wide variety of chain and

Traditional masks at Green Point Market

Unusual souvenirs

boutique stores are clustered under one roof. The best-known is the conveniently located V&A Waterfront, which has an excellent selection of shops catering specifically to tourists. Generally, the main chain stores are represented in the covered Victoria Wharf Shopping Mall, the largest building on the Waterfront, while souvenir and craft shops tend to be dotted between the outdoor bars and cafés. The huge Waterfront Craft Market is a fantastic source of high-quality items, while craftsmen in the Red Shed Craft Workshop will custom-make items to specification *in situ.*

Similar in scale but less tourist-oriented, Canal Walk Mall northeast of the city centre contains 400-odd shops, cinemas and restaurants, and is connected by shuttle bus to several popular hotels. Gardens Centre, the most popular mall in the city, hosts almost 100 boutique shops, chain stores and eateries. The newer Cape Quarter in fashionable De Waterkant has several crafts, jewellery, decor and art shops. The less trendy Golden Acre Mall in Adderley Street has seen better days, but it is conveniently central. The largest complex on the southern Cape Peninsula, Long Beach Mall near Noordhoek, contains at least 100 shops, supermarkets, shops, cinemas and eateries. Other large malls include Tygervalley in the northern suburbs and Claremont's Cavendish Square.

Although there are numerous shops selling African arts and crafts, you will generally find the same items in markets at much lower prices. Brightly coloured African fabrics abound at the flea market at Grand Parade, as do hand-crafted clothes, which you can also find at Greenmarket Square. Running southwards from Greenmarket Square, St George's Pedestrian Mall is lined with dozens of craft stalls and clothing and jewellery shops. Nearby Long Street is a particularly good source of second-hand books and antique clothing. The Pan-African Market, sprawling across three crammed storeys at 76 Long Street, has imported craftwork from all over Africa, along with local craftsmen, musicians and tailors, and a café serving local staples.

The market at Kirstenbosch National Botanical Gardens (last Sunday of every month, September–May) is notable for the quality crafts on offer. In the charming small towns along the Cape Peninsula you will find lots of local crafts and art, often of a very high standard, some sold from roadside stalls. Hout Bay and Noordhoek are known for their artists, sculptors and potters, whilst the Mariner's Wharf at Hout Bay boasts a shop specialising in maritime memorabilia, including shipwreck relics. Kalk Bay and Simon's Town are particularly well endowed with shops selling unusual gifts and art objects, and there is a regular craft market at Hermanus.

Many of the wineries sell not only their own wine,

A local boutique

but also gifts and/or gourmet foods. The towns along the Wine Routes can also be a good source of Cape Dutch collectables and antiques. Paarl has an Art and Craft Market on the first Saturday of each month and Stellenbosch has lots of craft boutiques and curio shops in its old town. If you travel to Stellenbosch, do not miss Oom Samie Se Winkel in Dorp Street. This remarkable emporium has remained virtually unchanged over the past 100 years, and is full of fascinating items.

ENTERTAINMENT

Cape Town has a cosmopolitan cultural milieu, with some excellent theatre and live music on offer, as well as one of the most vibrant nightlife scenes in Africa. The daily and weekly newspapers contain events listings which give guides to what's on, and it is definitely worth watching out for performances at unusual venues. Local radio station Good Hope FM is another good source of information, as is the Mail & Guardian's website – www.mg.co.za.

Theatre and Live Music

The premier venue for performing arts is the Artscape Complex (formerly the Nico Malan Theatre) in the city centre. With three auditoriums, this complex hosts a busy programme of classical music, ballet, opera, drama, light musicals and cabaret performances, and details of current and forthcoming performances are available at www.artscape.co.za.

The Baxter Theatre in Rosebank (www.baxter.co.za) presents contemporary music and dance. If your taste is for more traditional material, Shakespeare's plays can be seen in a romantic outdoor setting under the night sky at the Maynardville Open-Air Theatre (www.maynardville.co.za) in

Wynberg, during January and February. The Oude Libertas Arts Programme in Stellenbosch stages theatrical performances amongst the grapevines from January to March.

Live music can be heard at all the city's theatres. This ranges from classical to popular, and, increasingly, traditional and contemporary variations on African music. The Cape Town Philharmonic Orchestra plays at the Artscape Complex most weeks, and this venue also stages lunchtime and Sunday afternoon concerts. The Cape Town Symphony Orchestra plays each week at City Hall.

Try to take in one of the summer outdoor performances at the Kirstenbosch National Botanical Gardens or the Josephine Mill at Newlands, and enjoy picnicking and listening to music in beautiful surroundings. Other venues include the South African Museum and the Amphitheatre at the V&A Waterfront, which regularly puts on free concerts.

Live music can be heard in many of Cape Town's bars

Cape Town is renowned for its distinctive jazz, influenced by traditional African music and made most famous by Abdullah Ibrahim (known as 'Dollar Brand'). The Green Dolphin Restaurant (V&A Waterfront) and Dizzy's Cigar Bar and Pub (Camps Bay) are two notable live jazz venues, while Manenberg's Jazz Café on Adderley and Church streets often sees terrific performances of Cape township jazz.

Nightlife and Cinemas

Welcome to party town! Cape Town is known for its varied and vibrant nightlife – most clubs do not open until 11pm and are bound by law to close at 4am sharp. Many are open seven nights a week. A popular area is the V&A Waterfront, which tends to have the most conventional venues, while Long and Loop streets in the city centre attract the young and hip, who spend all night wandering between the enormous selection of pubs and clubs. Somerset Road and the surrounding areas of De Waterkant and Green Point are the main focal point of the gay scene.

Most of the major shopping malls have multi-screen cinemas that show the latest big Hollywood productions. Art cinemas include the Labia on Orange Street, the Baxter in Rondebosch and Cinema Nouveau in the Victoria Wharf Shopping Mall (V&A Waterfront).

A trendy bar on Long Street

SPORTS

Capetonians, like all South Africans, are mad about sports, both as spectators and participants. Cape Town's moderate climate means that many activities can be enjoyed year-round. The geography of the region is perfect for all kinds of outdoor pursuits, including swimming, watersports, fishing, horse-riding, cycling, golf and hiking.

Spectator Sports

The rugby and cricket stadia in Newlands, overlooked by the eastern slopes of Table Mountain, are home to the Western Cape's provincial rugby and cricket franchises, and both stadia regularly host key domestic and international fixtures. Rugby and cricketing standards are very high. The South African national side has won the Rugby World Cup twice in four starts (1995 and 2007), and the national cricket team is also considered to be one of the world's finest, with several of its leading players in recent years having hailed from the Western Cape, notably Jacques Kallis, Herschelle Gibbs and Gary Kirstin.

South Africa hosted the Rugby and Cricket World Cups in 1995 and 2003 respectively, and will follow this up by hosting the 2010 FIFA Football World Cup, making it the first country after the UK to achieve this prestigious sporting hat trick. The national football side, Bafana Bafana – The Boys! – has not shone as brightly as it might in recent years, but it is still ranked among the top sides in Africa.

Until the end of the 2004/5 season, Newlands Rugby Stadium was home to the city's leading football side, Ajax Cape Town, which plays in the South African Premium League during the southern winter. Several talented players started their career here before making their name in the English Premiership, notably Benni McCarthy, Steven Pienaar and Quinton

A close encounter

Fortune. Ajax Cape Town relocated to Athlone Stadium on the Cape Flats in 2005, and is also likely to play regular fixtures at the more central Green Point Stadium once it has been rebuilt for the 2010 World Cup. Details of forthcoming rugby, football and cricket fixtures can be found in the local press.

Horse-racing is another very popular spectator sport. There are three racetracks, at Durbanville, Kenilworth and Milnerton, and racehorses are bred at Robertson. The J&B Metropolitan Handicap, held each year at Kenilworth, is a highly prestigious sporting and social event, where the fashions worn by racegoers are almost as important as what is happening on the track.

Every March, Cape Town plays host to the famous Cape Argus Pick 'n' Pay Cycle Tour. Over 30,000 competitors, including many from overseas, race along a stunning 105km (65-mile) route around the Cape Peninsula. The sheer number of riders, plus the lavish costumes some wear, makes this a spectacular event to watch.

The city forms part of the route for many running marathons, the most important being the Puma Peninsula Marathon (February) and the 56km (35-mile) Two Oceans Marathon (Easter Saturday), both of which draw thousands of competitors from all around the world.

Cape Town is a popular stopping point for round-the-world yacht races. The South Atlantic (formerly Cape-to-Rio) Yacht Race leaves from here every two to three years, with the next due to leave for Salvador in January 2009.

Active Pursuits

Sports enthusiasts are spoilt for choice in Cape Town. Huge amounts of money have been invested in sporting facilities which are, almost without exception, excellent.

If you are keen on golf you'll be in paradise, with more than a dozen superb courses in glorious locations to choose from, including The Royal Cape at Wynberg, the country's oldest golf club, established in 1885. Most clubs welcome visitors on weekdays.

Horse-riding is another popular activity, and there are plenty of beautiful places to ride, including some beaches and vineyards. Mountain-biking offers another form of mounted transport. If you prefer to take your exercise on your own two feet, there are innumerable hiking trails throughout the national parks and reserves, and many hikers head for Table Mountain at weekends.

Kite-surfing at Muizenberg

The Outeniqua Choo-Tjoe route passes spectacular scenery

With so much coastline, it is not surprising that watersports-lovers are well catered for. Some of the best surfers in the world make their home in Cape Town, and there are surfing competitions at Kommetjie, while windsurfing is also popular. Scuba diving among the shipwrecks and kelp forests is a fascinating way to study the ecosystem off the Cape. Not all the beaches are suitable for swimming, either because of treacherous currents and pounding surf or because the water is too cold, but there are plenty of places where it is safe to swim *(see page 95)*.

The same combination of the warm Indian Ocean and cooler Atlantic that makes the waters so alluring to divers is responsible for the remarkable wealth of marine life that brings fishermen in their droves. Standing, fishing rod in hand, on a virtually deserted beach, with golden-white sand stretching as far as the eye can see, is an idyllic experience few forget. Deep-sea game fishermen can charter boats to seek out swordfish, marlin and yellowfin tuna.

Those with a sense of adventure can enjoy white-water rafting along the Breede or Berg rivers, leap off Lion's Head and paraglide over Cape Town, or go shark-cage diving off Dyer Island. If a more serene form of outdoor activity appeals, hot-air ballooning over the Winelands is probably the answer.

Scenic Train Journeys

A train journey provides an unusual way to see the Cape. Cape Town's local commuter rail operator, Metrorail (www.capemetrorail.co.za), operates several services of interest to tourists. A hop on hop off ticket is available for their southern route, which runs from Cape Town to Simon's Town, passing some fine scenery along the False Bay Coast. You can also have breakfast or lunch on board Biggsy's Restaurant Carriage and Wine Bar on this route (tel: 021-788 7760). Other services run out east to Stellenbosch and Strand, a resort on the south coast.

If you have a day to spare, opt for the Outeniqua Choo-Tjoe, the little steam train which runs through glorious surroundings between Mossel Bay and George (tel: 044-801 8288, www.onlinesources.co.za/chootjoe). Rovos Rail also operates some journeys between Cape Town and George in 1940s carriages (tel: 012-421 4020, www.rovos.co.za).

If budget and time are no problem, treat yourself to a trip on the legendary Blue Train, one of the most luxurious trains in the world, which runs between Cape Town and Pretoria (tel: 021-449 2672, www.blue train.co.za), or one of the epic journeys operated by Shongololo Express (tel: 011-483 0657, www.shongololo.com). This latter combines cross-country rail travel by night with daytime excursions by minibuses, carried on board the train, in a 4,500km (2,800-mile) trip from Cape Town to Johannesburg, via some of the top tourist destinations in South Africa.

If all this whets your appetite for vintage trains, check out the Outeniqua Railway Museum in George. Exhibits include the Emil Kessler – Johannesburg's first steam locomotive, a coach from the Royal Train of 1947 and Paul Kruger's private carriage.

Third Beach at the fashionable resort of Clifton

BEACHES

Cape Town's coastal suburbs boast unrivalled beaches, with
great stretches of clean, golden sand, some miles long, with the
ocean on one side and majestic mountains on the other.
Whether your preference is for sheltered coves or wild expanses
of unspoilt dunes for dozing in the sunshine, or tackling break-
ing waves on a surfboard, you will find a beach to suit you.

The beaches on the rugged Atlantic coast, which runs down
the western side of the peninsula, whilst perfect for walking
and sunbathing, aren't ideal for swimming, unless you're very
hardy. The water temperature is chilly, seldom rising above
15°C (59°F). Those on the False Bay seaboard, north and east
of Cape Point, have warmer waters, though some are over-
developed. The wind off the ocean can be a problem, whipping
up the fine sand into a stinging cloud, and the False Bay beaches are battered in summer by vicious southeasterly winds.

On the Atlantic coast, the closest beaches to the city centre are at Sea Point, but the sea is unsuitable for swimming here and the area generally unattractive. A little further south is the very fashionable resort of Clifton, with its anchorage of expensive yachts. It has four small beaches, all sandy, sheltered and extremely popular with the young and beautiful. Swimming is safe, but the water painfully cold. Parking is a nightmare (don't even try in the peak summer season), but there are regular buses from the city centre.

Camps Bay, a mile or so south of Clifton, is another fashionable residential suburb, with fantastic views of Lion's Head, the Twelve Apostles mountains and the Atlantic Ocean. The broad beach attracts families, and the town has many lively and affordable restaurants and cafés.

The stunning beach at Llandudno, 20km (12 miles) south of Cape Town, is a fabulous, sheltered cove set at the foot of a mountain, with giant boulders dominating the landscape. Sunsets are memorable, sunbathing idyllic and the surf highly dangerous. A 20-minute walk from Llandudno is Sandy Bay, the main nudist beach for Cape Town. Accessible only by walking, it is an exceptionally pretty spot, with wild flowers and sand dunes, though nude sunbathing can be a painful experience when the wind off the ocean blows the sand around in great clouds!

Noordhoek, at the end of the thrilling journey along Chapman's Peak Drive, is incredibly impressive, with smooth white sand stretching for over 6km (3.7 miles). Swimming can be hazardous off this gloriously wild beach, which is very popular with horse-riders, but walking along its vast shoreline is a relaxing experience to be cherished.

The water in the small basin at Kommetjie, a 15km (9-mile) drive from Noordhoek, is wonderful for swimming, the temperature here a little higher than the ocean. Surfers tackle the breakers at Long Beach, the site of serious surfing competitions.

Sunscreen is essential wear

The beaches in the Cape of Good Hope Nature Reserve are great for windswept walks, but few are suitable for swimming, though some have safe tidal pools.

Swimming is safe in the cove at Smitswinkelbaai on the False Bay coast, but the beach is accessible only by walking down a vast number of steps. Miller's Point has several sandy beaches and rare wildlife, including black zonure lizards, but 5km (3 miles) north lies one of the most popular areas on the False Bay seaboard, Boulders. As the name implies, this series of small beaches is distinguished by numerous massive rocks, but its real claim to fame is the community of endangered African penguins which live here in a protected reserve on the beach. The combination of beautiful beach, crystal-clear rock pools, warm water and these wonderful black-and-white birds, which love to mingle with the bathers, is irresistible to tens of thousands of tourists every year.

Fish Hoek has a superb family beach, with safe swimming and good facilities, while Muizenberg, northeast of Fish Hoek on the M4, is overcrowded and faded, but its beach is still immensely popular, and there are plenty of family seaside activities like miniature golf.

The most popular beaches generally all have parking lots, but in high season it can be virtually impossible to find space. Those along the False Bay seaboard are well served by trains from Cape Town, and at the busiest times this is also the quickest way to get there.

CHILDREN'S CAPE TOWN

Like all of South Africa, Cape Town is generally very welcoming to children, and there is plenty to keep the kids entertained. The beaches are a huge family attraction, and most children are thrilled by the ride to the top of Table Mountain and the chance to spot baboons at the summit. Older children who really want to understand some of the history of South Africa should find a trip to Robben Island thought-provoking and moving.

Many of the museums and exhibitions are geared to entertain younger visitors, notably the South African Museum, with its hands-on Discovery Room and fascinating Whale Well. The adjoining Planetarium offers regular children's shows. In Rosebank in the Southern Suburbs, the Baxter has a very good children's theatre.

Beside the tidal pool at Camps Bay

Wildlife at the Victoria and Alfred Waterfront

The V&A Waterfront has lots to offer kids. The floating exhibits at the South African National Maritime Museum are great fun to explore. Kids can also scrabble for semi-precious stones at the Scratch Patch on Dock Road and literally get to grips with life under the sea in the touch tanks of the Two Oceans Aquarium.

The penguins at Boulders Beach are popular with the children, and even the most blasé teenager cannot help but be impressed by the majestic sight of whales at Hermanus. Other popular animal attractions include Hout Bay's World of Birds, Africa's largest bird park, and Tygerberg Zoo, situated in the Winelands, which is the only one in the Cape Town area.

Other child-friendly attractions in the Winelands include the self-explanatory Butterfly World and Drakenstein Lion Park. For wine-lovers with children, there is no better place to head for than the Spirit Wine Estate south of Stellenbosch, which boasts two excellent playgrounds as well as features such as tame cheetahs, a birds of prey centre and pony rides.

Children suffering withdrawal symptoms from theme parks will enjoy Ratanga Junction, at Century City. South Africa's first major theme park, it offers entertainment for the whole family. Rides include the huge, bright-yellow Cobra rollercoaster and Crocodile Gorge. There are gentler rides for the tinies, plus 'jungle cruises'.

Calendar of Events

There are so many exciting activities happening in and around Cape Town throughout the year that it would be impossible to cover them all in this guide. Cape Town Tourism and the various regional tourist boards will have full listings *(see page 126)*.

January Kaapse Klopse (Cape Minstrel Carnival), Cape Town (1–2 January); South Atlantic Yacht Race, Cape Town (every two to three years), J&B Metropolitan Handicap, Kenilworth.

February Dias Festival, Mossel Bay; Puma Peninsula Marathon; Cape Town Gay Pride Festival (city centre).

March Cape Argus Pick 'n' Pay Cycle Tour; Stellenbosch Wine Festival; Cape Town Festival (music, drama and other arts performances); Cape Town International Jazz Festival; Western Cape Yellowfin Challenge, Hout Bay; Nederburg Wine Auction, Paarl; end of Spier and Oude Libertas festivals near Stellenbosch.

April Two Oceans Marathon, Cape Town (Easter Saturday); Franschhoek Festival.

May Whale-watching begins.

June Snoek Festival, Hout Bay.

July Bastille Festival, Franschhoek; Knysna Oyster Festival, Berg River Canoe Marathon, Paarl; Port Festival, Calitzdorp.

August Stellenbosch Wine Festival; Calamari Festival, Plettenberg Bay; Lipton Cup Yacht Race, Cape Town; Hout Bay Festival.

September Darling Art Festival; Darling Wild Flower and Orchid Show; Fernkloof Wild Flower Show, Hermanus; Whale Festival, Hermanus; Spring Flower Show, Kirstenbosch National Botanical Gardens; Stellenbosch Festival.

October Food and Wine Festival, Stellenbosch; Oudtshoorn Ostrich Festival; Spring Regatta, Table Bay.

November Fireworks Festival, Saldanha; Winelands Marathon, Stellenbosch; start of Spier and Oude Libertas festivals near Stellenbosch.

December Christmas Carols, Greenmarket Square; Crayfish Festival, Lambert's Bay; Rothmans Week Sailing Regatta, Table Bay.

EATING OUT

Even the choosiest eaters will find something to suit their appetite in Cape Town. The city is famed for the quality and range of its cuisine, and it is remarkably easy to eat out well without blowing the holiday budget.

Whether you want a tasty snack in an informal bistro or an elegant candlelit dinner in sumptuous surroundings, you will find it in and around Cape Town. The V&A Waterfront alone is home to a vast range of eateries to suit all tastes and pockets, while the Southern Suburbs and Winelands towns – Franschhoek in particular – boast many fine restaurants, often in superb old Cape Dutch buildings. Saturday morning breakfast at one of the cafés that line Greenmarket Square, serenaded by buskers, has become a Cape Town tradition.

As befits a cosmopolitan city, the cuisine of many countries is available, including Chinese, French, Greek, Italian, Indian, Japanese, Thai and Turkish. Restaurants offering traditional food from other parts of Africa are on the increase.

Picnicking

With the excellent climate and glorious beaches and countryside close at hand, picnics are popular. Many beaches have dedicated picnic areas, and excellent, easily portable food can be bought from delicatessens. Some hotels will prepare picnics for their guests, and the vineyards will often sell filled picnic baskets, to be enjoyed in their grounds.

When to Eat

Breakfast is available from coffee shops from about 9am (though many open earlier in the city centre), and lingering over a hearty breakfast while watching the world go by is a good start to a day's sightseeing. Afternoon tea is served at certain hotels and coffee shops, while most restaurants offer both lunch and dinner, with dinner gen-

Dining out in the city centre

erally served from 6.30pm until about 10pm, though in areas such as the V&A Waterfront they may be open later.

It is worth checking the opening times in advance, to avoid disappointment. Also remember not all restaurants are open every day. The most popular can sometimes be fully booked for weeks in advance, so securing a table can be a problem if you are on a short holiday, unless you book before you travel.

Cape Malay Cuisine

The city's history can be traced through its food. Dutch, English, French, German and Portuguese culinary influences have all played a part, but the most significant is that of the 'Malay' slaves who came from the East Indies in the 17th century.

Local Cape Malay specialities include *bobotie*, a sweetish curried minced lamb served with a topping of baked savoury custard; *sosaties*, a sort of marinated kebab; *bredie*, a spicy stew traditionally made from venison or mutton and often

Delicious seafood sushi

accompanied by a sweetened vegetable or fruit dish, and *smoorsnoek*, lightly curried snoek, a local line fish.

Restaurants specialising in this cuisine are few and far between, but there is no finer exponent than the award-winning historic Cellars-Hohenort Hotel, adjacent to Kirstenbosch Botanical Gardens. However, Cape Malay dishes can be found on the wider menus of many restaurants, so it is not difficult to sample this local fare. For a treat, head for Cape Colony in the Mount Nelson Hotel.

Stunning Seafood

As might be expected of a city surrounded by largely un-developed ocean frontage, Cape Town is renowned for its excellent fresh seafood, which is the speciality of perhaps half the city's leading restaurants. For reliable but inexpensive seafood, Ocean Basket is a popular seafood bistro chain, represented at the V&A Waterfront among other locations, and offering a varied menu in friendly, unpretentious surroundings.

At more upmarket eateries, the choice and quality of fresh seafood can be outstanding. Shellfish, including crayfish, lobster, oysters (often served with hot chilli sauce) and mussels, are in plentiful supply, as are the extremely tasty linefish, including snoek, yellowtail, kingklip, kabeljou and geelbek. Since the Russians decimated the Mozambique prawn beds with overfishing, prawns have tended to be expensive.

South Africans love to *braai* – barbecue – and seafood lends itself particularly well to this form of cooking. If you are fond of fish, try to make the time to head along the coastal roads to of one of the open-air seafood restaurants, especially Die Strandloper on the beach at Langebaan. Here you get the chance, over a 10-course meal, to taste the freshest seafood the Western Cape has to offer.

Meat, Meat… and More Meat

Most South Africans are great meat-eaters, and the range on offer is impressive. Menus are often supplemented by more unusual varieties, including ostrich and crocodile.

Steak remains one of the most common choices, often accompanied by monkey-gland sauce (a sort of chutney) or a more fiery Madagascan green pepper sauce. Fries are the most common accompaniment, though baked potatoes and rice may also be offered, together with a selection of vegetables. Steakhouse chains such as Spurs are a good option for those on tighter budgets or travelling with children.

A traditional *braai*

The influence of German settlers can be seen in the range of highly spiced *boerewors* ('farmer's sausages') that are available.

Biltong, dried meat, is a South African speciality which evolved centuries ago when meat could best be preserved by spicing, salting and drying. Beef biltong is the most common, but it is also made from game. It can be bought packaged in strips, and is increasingly to be found on restaurant menus, usually shaved over salad. Trying it is a must, but it is not to everyone's taste!

Breakfast Afrikaans-style is a hearty affair, often including many eggs, several rashers of bacon, plus steak. Don't panic if you can't face such huge feasts; it is equally easy to start the day with muffins or fresh fruit.

Vegetarians need not despair. A huge selection of fresh salads and vegetables are available all year round, with most menus offering vegetarian options. If you can't locate a specialist vegetarian restaurant, Indian restaurants are well represented and always offer a great selection of meat-free dishes.

Rooibos Tea

Don't leave Cape Town without trying one of the indigenous specialities – rooibos tea. This remarkably versatile product was first discovered over 100 years ago, by the Coloured population of the Cederberg area. They picked the wild *Aspalanthus linearis*, known as rooibos ('red bush'), and bruised the leaves with hammers before drying them in the sun and making a refreshing tea-like drink.

In 1905 a Russian immigrant, Benjamin Ginsberg, began to exploit its potential, and by the 1930s Clanwilliam had become the centre of production. Today it is drunk throughout South Africa and exported around the world. It is low in tannin and free of caffeine, so very good for you. It is alleged to help those suffering from insomnia, indigestion, hay fever and even nappy rash (applied, cold, to the skin in this last case!). It can also be used for cooking, incorporated into soups, cakes, stews, and all manner of hot and cold drinks.

Visitors to Clanwilliam, an elegant old town in the shadow of the Cederberg Mountains, can tour the vast fields of rooibos and see the processing sheds. Rooibos recipes can be found at www.rooibosltd.co.za.

Desserts

Local delicacies include *malva*, made from cream, sugar and apricot conserve, and Cape brandy pudding, a steamed pudding soaked with brandy. Equally tasty, but less guilt-inducing, are fresh fruit kebabs. If you don't have a sweet tooth, South African cheeses are very good, and you will usually be offered local versions of the European classics such as brie.

Iced rooibos tea

What to Drink

South Africa is the world's ninth-largest wine producer, with almost 600 wineries producing around 900 million litres (nearly 200 million gallons) annually, a mere 40 percent of which is consumed locally, ensuring that local prices remain very competitive even as exports soar. The industry is concentrated almost exclusively in the Western Cape, spreading outwards from traditional centres such as Constantia, Stellenbosch, Franschhoek and Paarl into newer areas such as the Breede and Olifants river valleys.

In terms of acreage, white grapes predominate, with Chenin Blanc, Columbard (used mainly for brandy), Chardonnay and Sauvignon Blanc respectively accounting for around 19 percent, 11 percent, 8 percent and 7½ percent of the national vineyard area. The leading red, both in terms of prestige and acreage, is Cabernet Sauvignon, which covers 13 percent of the vineyard area, and tends to produce wines that are well suited to cellaring, often blended with Shiraz or Merlot (which account for 9 percent and 7 percent of the vineyard area respectively). For something different, however, it is often worth choosing a Pinotage, a grape that is unique to South Africa and as a result often underrated and very well priced. Many other varietals well known to international wine-lovers, for instance Pinot Noir, Cabernet Franc and Semillon, are poorly represented in South Africa, though this is changing. If you are thinking of buying to cellar, the best of recent vintages for serious reds were 2003 and to a lesser extent 2006.

Not all restaurants have alcohol licences, but the Cape is so steeped in wine culture that it is common practice to bring your own wine, even to the most upmarket eatery, and corkage is usually either not charged, or very low.

Lager is also a popular choice, usually served very cold, and microbreweries are emerging, including Mitchell's at the V&A Waterfront. For non-drinkers, there is a vast choice of fresh fruit juices, including apricot, guava and pear.

Take your pick from the wide range of fine wines on offer

HANDY TRAVEL TIPS

An A–Z Summary of Practical Information

A Accommodation .. 108
  Airport 109
B Budgeting for
    Your Trip 109
C Camping 110
  Car Hire 110
  Climate 111
  Clothing 112
  Crime and
    Safety 112
  Customs and Entry
    Requirements ... 113
D Driving 114
E Electricity 116
  Embassies and
    Consulates 116
  Emergencies 116
G Gay and Lesbian
    Travellers 116
  Getting There 117
  Guides and
    Tours 118

H Health and
    Medical Care ... 118
  Holidays 119
L Language 120
M Maps 121
  Media 121
  Money 122
O Opening Hours ... 122
P Police 122
  Post Offices 123
  Public Transport ... 123
R Religion 124
T Telephones 124
  Tickets 125
  Time Zones 125
  Tipping 125
  Toilets 126
  Tourist Information . 126
W Websites 126
  Weights and
    Measures 127
Y Youth Hostels 127

A

ACCOMMODATION *(see also* CAMPING, YOUTH HOSTELS *and* RECOMMENDED HOTELS *on pages* 128–34)

Cape Town and its environs offer accommodation of all standards and prices, from simple backpackers' hostels to five-star luxury hotels. The Tourism Grading Council of South Africa (TGCSA) operates a one- to five-star grading system for accommodation, but many fine B&Bs opt not to participate.

Advance booking is essential during peak season (November–April), particularly during the South African school summer holidays (early December to mid-January), when prices can rise by up to 50 percent. Cape Town and Western Cape Tourism *(see page 126)* operates a free booking service through its local information offices and has excellent accommodation listings at www.tourismcapetown.co.za.

Throughout the Western Cape you will encounter extremely well-run small independent hotels, often in quiet locations with beautiful gardens. The area is also well endowed with fine guest houses and B&Bs. Many are in elegant old gabled Cape Dutch houses, and offer excellent value. Guest House Accommodation of Southern Africa (GHASA) supplies information and has a useful online booking service www.ghasa.co.za. In addition, self-catering cottages, often in stunning locations, are available to rent by the sea or on farms.

The V&A Waterfront area is an enjoyable place to stay in the city centre. The main hotels here are set slightly away from the busy nightlife spots, so it is not too noisy, and many of the restaurants are open later than others in Cape Town. The historic city centre is virtually deserted at night; arguably uncomfortably so, while the Southern Suburbs are an excellent source of quiet, comfortable hotels in safe areas within easy striking distance of the city centre's attractions.

Many of the expensive hotels in Cape Town and around the Western Cape often will not accept children aged under 12.

AIRPORT

Cape Town's International Airport (tel: 021-937 1200; www.acsa. co.za) flanks the N2 highway 22km (13 miles) east of the city centre. It has a bureau de change, duty-free facilities, car rental offices, hotel booking kiosks and a VAT refund office.

There are no trains to and from the airport, but some upmarket hotels operate shuttle services, and almost all hotels will arrange transfers to or from the airport in advance. Randy's Tours (tel: 021-706 0166; www.randystours.com) operates a regular shuttle to the city centre, V&A Waterfront, Green Point and Camps Bay at R60–170 per person depending on destination and group size. Private taxis are available at a higher price (tel: 021-919 4659).

The airport has an isolated location and the only nearby hotel – within walking distance – is the inexpensive and well-equipped CTIA Road Lodge (tel: 021-934 7303; www.citylodge.co.za).

B

BUDGETING FOR YOUR TRIP

Favourable exchange rates mean that it is easy to enjoy high-quality accommodation and catering without spending a fortune.

Air fares. These vary hugely, according to the time of year. April and May are usually the cheapest times to fly, and December and January the most expensive. Round-trip flights from the US can cost in the region of $1,200–2,200 (low season–high season), from the UK or Europe about £600–1,000, and from Australia A$1,750–2,000. Package tours may reduce the costs significantly.

Accommodation. A double room in a luxurious four- to five-star hotel will cost anywhere between R1,500–3,000 per night. A good two- to three-star hotel might charge R800–1,500 for a double, while B&Bs charge anything between R500–1,000, with major discounts available across the board in the local winter (May–September). Breakfast is generally included in the room price.

Meals and drinks. An average three-course meal costs R150–300, a bottle of wine in a restaurant R60–150 and a cup of tea R5–10.

Sightseeing. Many museums and galleries charge a nominal entry fee and a few offer free admission. National parks and reserves charge higher fees, and activities such as the Table Mountain Cableway and guided tours to Robben Island are relatively pricey.

Taxis. A trip in one of the tourist-friendly Rikkis should cost R12–20. Metered taxis charge about R8–10 per kilometre.

C

CAMPING

There is a good network of campsites in the rural areas and national parks around Cape Town. Private resorts are much better than the municipal campsites, in terms of washing and cooking facilities and safety, while rough camping simply isn't safe. Private resorts often have shops, cafés, barbecue stands and a swimming pool.

CAR HIRE (see also DRIVING)

Though public transport in Cape Town is amongst the best in South Africa, the story is not always the same outside the city. With so many magnificent destinations to travel to, a car is invaluable.

Cars can be rented from desks at the airport and rental offices in the city. There are many in Cape Town, including Avis (tel: 021-934 0330; www.avis.co.za), Budget (tel: 021-934 3180; www.budget. co.za), Dollar Thrifty (tel: 021-934 0266; www.thrifty.co.za), Europcar (tel: 021-934 4750; www.europcar.co.za) and Hertz (tel: 021-934 3913; www.ecom.hertz.co.za).

Car rental is not cheap, but rivalry between the big international names and smaller local organisations ensures that there are good deals to be had if you shop around. Local firms are generally cheaper, but if you decide to rent a car through one of the international names, you can pick it up in one city and deposit it in another.

Check that the rental includes collision damage and theft waivers, and breakdown and accident rescue, and be aware that some insurance does not include dirt roads. With so much to see around Cape Town, unlimited mileage is a sensible option. Some companies offer very good deals which include a mobile phone on which one can make and receive international calls, with no charge for incoming calls.

If your driving licence isn't printed in English or doesn't bear your photograph, you will need an International Driving Permit to rent a car, which you must obtain before you arrive in South Africa. Most companies insist on the driver being aged at least 21, with some stipulating a minimum age of 23 or even 25.

Motorhome rental is big business in Cape Town. It is a great way to travel to remote places, using the excellent campsites in national parks. Although you'll save on accommodation, it is not a cheap option. Rental is usually fairly high, as is petrol consumption. Most petrol stations only take cash, so you may have to carry large amounts of money to remote areas. Motorhome rental companies with offices in the city include Britz Africa (www.britz.co.za) and Rainbow Camper Hire (www.rainbowcamperhire.co.za). Knysna Camper Hire (tel: 044-384 0141) is a good rental company on the Garden Route.

CLIMATE

South Africa's climate is the reverse of that of the northern hemisphere, with midwinter in June and July and high summer in December and January. It is always a few degrees cooler by the coast than inland. Cape Town has a Mediterranean climate, with cool, wet winters and warm to hot, dry summers. Autumn (March–May) and Spring (September–November) are the wettest seasons, with short periods of heavy rain. Though the climate is temperate, it is liable to change suddenly, switching from bright sunshine to grey skies within minutes.

The chart below gives Cape Town's average minimum and maximum temperatures.

	J	F	M	A	M	J	J	A	S	O	N	D
Max												
°C	26	27	26	23	20	18	17	18	19	21	24	25
°F	79	80	79	74	68	64	63	64	66	70	75	77
Min												
°C	16	16	15	13	11	9	8	9	10	12	14	15
°F	61	61	59	55	52	48	46	48	50	54	57	59

CLOTHING

Informal clothing is generally accepted everywhere, though most restaurants prefer smart casual dress, and a few very posh places might require men to wear a jacket and tie, particularly after 6pm. Always be prepared for the weather to change. Even in high summer it is advisable to take a jacket or sweater with you for sudden drops in temperature, or to wear on boat trips. Comfortable shoes are invaluable for hikes through forests or national parks.

CRIME AND SAFETY

The usual rules of self-preservation which apply in any major city should be followed with extra vigilance in Cape Town. The golden rule is to be sensible and be aware of what is happening around you.

Do not walk alone after dark, and never display expensive jewellery or cameras. If you think you are being followed, change direction or vary your pace. When returning to your hotel after dark, always use the main entrance, and avoid unlit places.

Use credit cards and travellers' cheques, and keep the amount of cash you carry to a minimum. Watch out for groups of small children surrounding you, and don't carry valuables in easily accessible pockets. If the worst happens and you are mugged, remain calm and do not resist, as guns are all too common.

When travelling by car, be aware that car-jacking is on the increase in Cape Town. Again, there are obvious precautions to take:

keep doors locked and shut all windows whenever the car has to stop; plan your route in advance and make long journeys during daylight only; store personal items out of sight; park only in well-lit areas, and never pick up hitchhikers.

Never venture into the Cape Flats townships unless on a guided tour. Most crime is centred on areas tourists seldom visit, while areas such as the Garden Route and Little Karoo are extremely safe.

CUSTOMS AND ENTRY REQUIREMENTS

All visitors to South Africa need a passport valid for at least six months. Citizens of the US, EU, Australia, Canada and New Zealand currently do not need a visa. As regulations are subject to change, it is a good idea to check with your travel agent.

You will need a valid return ticket, or you must be able to show that you have the funds to buy one, and, if asked, you must be able to prove that you can support yourself while in the country.

Duty-free allowance. Travellers aged 18 and over are allowed to bring in 400 cigarettes, 250 grams of tobacco and 50 cigars, 1 litre of spirits, 2 litres of wine, 50ml of perfume and 250ml of toilet water, plus gifts and other souvenirs up to the value of R500. Duty is levied at 20 percent over these allowances.

VAT is charged at 14 percent. However, foreign tourists can re-claim the VAT they pay on goods with a total value of more than R250. The VAT Refund Office is based at Cape Town International Airport. You will need your passport and the original receipt, and may have to fill out a reclamation form. You must be able to produce the goods, if asked, or the money will not be refunded. There is an administration charge equivalent to 2 percent of the VAT paid, and refunds can be made in any currency.

Currency. There is no limit to the amount of local or foreign currency or travellers' cheques you can import, but exporting rand is limited to R5,000 in notes, and any excess must be reconverted before you leave the country.

D

DRIVING (see also CRIME AND SAFETY)

Road conditions. With its excellent network of roads and light traffic, driving in South Africa can be very enjoyable. The road surfaces are generally good, with wide hard shoulders. However, these same conditions also encourage recklessness, and the country has an unenviable accident record, with drink-driving and badly loaded, unstable vehicles among the causes. Another hazard on the road to watch out for is animals, particularly at night in country areas, so heed the warning signs.

Minibus taxis have an unwritten right of way, and they also frequently jump red lights. Their drivers often carry handguns, so it is not a good idea to object to their driving if you encounter one.

You may find overtaking drivers coming towards you, who may assume that you will move onto the hard shoulder to avoid an accident.

Rules and regulations. Foreign drivers' licences, printed in English and with a photograph, are valid in South Africa for up to six months. Other drivers must obtain an International Driving Permit. You must have your driver's licence with you at all times while driving.

South Africans drive on the left-hand side of the road, and speed limits are 60km/h (37mph) in built-up areas, 100km/h (60mph) on country roads and 120km/h (73mph) on major highways. Though there are heavy fines for those caught exceeding these limits, Capetonians frequently do so. Drivers and front-seat passengers are compelled by law to wear a seat belt.

There are few roundabouts, but you may encounter four-way stops. The person who gets to a stop sign first has right of way over drivers arriving at the other stops. At roundabouts and other junctions, give way to traffic coming from the right. Be aware that Capetonians tend to jump red lights.

Fuel costs. Compared to European prices, fuel is fairly cheap in Cape Town, though recent hikes in the oil price have pushed it to around US$1 per litre. There are plenty of filling stations on the main roads, but far less when you venture off the beaten track. Many will be open 24 hours in the city centre and between 7am–7pm in other urban areas. Opening hours can be much shorter in rural areas, so be sure to fill up when you get the opportunity. In most cases cash is the only form of payment accepted.

Parking. There are a good number of car parks in Cape Town, and lots of parking meters. You will also see many self-proclaimed 'parking attendants', who will, in return for a small payment, guide you to a parking space, then guard your car while you are away. If you are not happy with this idea, don't be intimidated; you are not compelled to park where they say. If you do decide use their services, however, insist on paying when you return to your car, as you have no guarantees that they will stay with your car if you pay in advance.

It is illegal to park on the opposite side of the road facing the on-coming traffic.

If you need help. If you are involved in an accident where no one is injured, you must inform the police within 24 hours. If someone is hurt, you must not move the vehicles until the police have arrived. Swap names and insurance details with the driver of the other vehicle.

If your car breaks down, pull in to the left and put a red warning triangle 50m (about 160ft) behind the car. The Automobile Association of South Africa can be called upon for advice and emergency rescue (tel: 083-84322), and may have a reciprocal arrangement with a driving association in your own country.

Road signs. Road signs are generally in both English and Afrikaans. Occasionally they will only be in Afrikaans, so make sure you know the name of your destination in that language. For example, Cape Town is Kaapstad. When travelling on dirt roads, be aware that it is easy to become slightly disoriented, and think you have travelled further than you have. If you are expecting a destination to be signed, wait until you see that sign until you turn off. Do not head off on any unsigned roads you may reach before.

E

ELECTRICITY

The power supply is 220/240 volts at 50 cycles per second (Hz). Most hotels have 110-volt sockets for electric razors. Take a three-point, round-pinned adaptor for hairdryers, etc, though they are readily available to buy if you forget.

EMBASSIES AND CONSULATES

Most embassies are in Pretoria, but many countries have consulates in Cape Town.

Australia: not represented; contact the high commission in Pretoria; 292 Orient Street; tel: 012-423 6000.

Canada: 19th Floor, SA Reserve Bank Building, 60 St George's Mall; tel: 021-423 5240.

Ireland: 12th Floor, LG Building, 1 Thibault Square, Long Street; tel: 021-419 0636/7.

New Zealand: 4 Kirstenbosch Drive, Bishopscourt; tel: 021-488 2425.

UK: 15th Floor, Southern Life Building, 8 Riebeeck Street; tel: 021-405 2400.

US: 7th Floor, Monte Carlo Building, Herengracht Street; tel: 021-702 7300.

EMERGENCIES

Ambulance: tel: **10177**
Police Flying Squad: tel: **10111**
Fire Brigade: tel: **021-535 1100**

G

GAY AND LESBIAN TRAVELLERS

Cape Town welcomes gay and lesbian travellers. South Africa has a progressive, gay- and lesbian-friendly constitution, and the city is the gay capital of the country. There are many gay clubs and restaurants, and an annual drag ball, held in December or January. Useful information is available through the Pink Guide (available from tourist offices) and Gay Net (tel: 021-422 1925; www.gaynetcapetown.co.za). Bear in mind that open displays of affection between gay couples are less tolerated in rural areas.

GETTING THERE

By air. There are an increasing number of direct flights to Cape Town International Airport from major European and US cities, including London, Atlanta and New York. Some travellers may still need to travel via Johannesburg.

High season (September–March, but especially December and January) is the most expensive time to travel, while winter and spring (April–October) is the cheapest.

Many tour operators offer package tours from North America, Europe or the UK. These tours can be all-inclusive, covering everything from flights, accommodation, car hire or local transport, meals and excursions to areas such as the Garden Route and Winelands. They can represent significant savings on booking all elements individually, though you may find yourself tied in to a group itinerary. London-based specialist operators such as Expert Africa (tel: +44 20 8232 9777; www.expertafrica.com) and Rainbow Tours (tel: +44 20 7227 1002; www.rainbowtours.co.uk) will tailor-make holidays for individuals with a less restricted budget, preparing itineraries to suit the specific interests of their clients.

Fly-drive deals are also available through many airlines in conjunction with international car rental companies.

By rail. Trains operate daily to Cape Town from other parts of South Africa, covering vast distances in journeys which can last up to 24 hours. A popular, if expensive, option is to travel to Cape Town from elsewhere in South Africa on one of the famous luxury trains which offer an irresistible combination of lavish accommodation and glorious, ever-changing scenery. The best-known of these is the Blue Train, which journeys between Cape Town and Pretoria (see also page 93).

By sea. As befits a destination with a such a long association with seafarers, Cape Town is on the route for a number of cruise lines, and it is also possible to travel as a passenger on board a cargo ship. The skyline has obviously changed dramatically since Bartolomeu Dias first ordered his ship steered in the direction of Table Mountain, but arriving by sea is still memorable.

GUIDES AND TOURS

Innumerable tour companies operate in the region, offering anything from a half-day tour of the V&A Waterfront or historic city centre, to trips along the Garden Route or Western Coast lasting over a week. All tour guides speak English, and many will also speak French, German or Spanish. Certain areas, such as the Cape Flats, should only be visited as part of a tour party, while only official tours are allowed to land on Robben Island.

Legend Tours (tel: 021-704 9140; www.legendtours.co.za) will take you around Bo-Kaap, District Six, Cape Flats and Robben Island. Flamingo Adventure Tours offer tours for disabled travellers and their companions to all major attractions (tel: 021-557 4496; www.flamingotours.co.za). Book Cape Town (tel: 021-422 5092; www.bookcapetown.com) offers a wide variety of day tours focused on wine, food, heritage or wildlife.

H

HEALTH AND MEDICAL CARE

Cape Town has excellent medical services. Doctors are listed in the telephone directory under 'Medical Practitioners', and hotels will usually call one for a guest, if required. Although patients are generally referred to a hospital by a doctor, in an emergency head straight for the casualty department of the nearest hospital. Outpatient treatment is available at relatively low cost, though you should take out medical insurance before you travel.

The biggest hospital in Cape Town is Groote Schuur (Hospital Drive, Observatory; tel: 021-404 9111). The world's first heart transplant operation took place here, in 1967. City Park Hospital on the corner of Longmarket and Bree streets is conveniently near the historic city centre (tel: 021-480 6111). Somerset Hospital on Beach Road, Mouille Point, also has outpatient and emergency departments (tel: 021-402 6911), and is convenient from the V&A Waterfront.

Pharmacies. Consult the Yellow Pages for the pharmacy closest to you. Not all pharmacies are open outside regular shopping hours, but those with extended opening hours include Hypermed Pharmacy, York Road and Main Road, Green Point (tel: 021-434 1414), open 8.30am–7pm Monday–Saturday, and 9am–7pm Sunday; and M-Kem on Durban Road next to the N1 highway (tel: 021-948 5706), the city's only 24-hour pharmacy.

No inoculations are mandatory for travel to anywhere in South Africa. It is, however, advisable to make sure that your tetanus and polio vaccinations are current.

Stomach upsets are rare as tap water is safe to drink, and ice and salad in restaurants are also safe. Malaria, though seasonally present along the northeastern coastal belt of South Africa and a few other border areas, is totally absent from the Western Cape. The greatest hazard to tourists is the African sun. Skin cancer is on the increase, so using a strong sunscreen and wearing a sun hat are essential. It is easy to burn as there is often a gentle breeze, so the scorching sun can feel deceptively cool. Rabies is present in the area, so assume the worst if you are bitten by an animal and go to hospital for treatment.

HOLIDAYS

1 January	New Year's Day
21 March	Human Rights Day
Good Friday	(movable)

Easter Sunday	(movable)
Family Day	(Easter Monday – movable)
27 April	Freedom Day
1 May	Workers' Day
16 June	Youth Day
9 August	National Women's Day
24 September	Heritage Day
16 December	Day of Reconciliation
25 December	Christmas Day
26 December	Day of Goodwill

L

LANGUAGE

There are 11 official languages in South Africa, with the three most common in the Western Cape being Afrikaans, English and Xhosa. English is the language of administration, so almost everyone speaks it, at least to some degree. Afrikaans is very closely related to Dutch. The 'g' is pronounced with a guttural 'kh', 'oe' is pronounced 'oo', 'v' is pronounced 'f', and 'w' is usually pronounced 'v'.

If you want to try some Afrikaans, the following phrases and vocabulary will be useful:

Good morning	**Goeie môre**
Good afternoon	**Goeie middag**
Good night	**Goeie nag**
Goodbye	**Tot siens**
Please	**Asseblief**
Thank you	**Dankie**
How much…?	**Hoeveel…?**
What is the time?	**Hoe laat is dit?**
Where is…?	**Waar is…?**

one	**een**	six	**ses**
two	**twee**	seven	**sewe**
three	**drie**	eight	**agt**
four	**vier**	nine	**nege**
five	**vyf**	ten	**tien**

MAPS

Western Cape Tourism *(see page 126)* can provide very good maps, usually free of charge. In addition, more detailed commercially produced maps, available at most bookshops, may be useful for those who plan to head off the main routes and explore the dirt roads.

MEDIA

Radio and television. The three state television channels, run by the South African Broadcasting Corporation (SABC) are known as SABC 1, 2 and 3. SABC 1 broadcasts almost entirely in English, and puts out a mix of soap operas, news, documentaries, game shows and American imports, and the other two channels broadcast a mixture of several languages. There is also an independent broadcaster called e.tv. Most hotels are tuned into the English-language satellite network DSTV, whose flagship M-Net is supplemented by international channels such as CNN, NTV, BBC Prime and Supersport.

The English-language SAFM radio station provides good morning and evening news programmes.

Newspapers. Newspapers are published in English and Afrikaans. National English-language newspapers include the *Sowetan* and *Star* (both daily), the *Sunday Times* and the weekly *Mail & Guardian*. *Business Day* is a financial daily, and the *Cape Times* and *Cape Argus* are local English-language dailies. CNA newsagents sell international publications including *Newsweek, Time* and *Weekly Telegraph*.

MONEY

Currency. The South African currency, the rand, is divided into 100 cents. R200, R100, R50, R20 and R10 banknotes are issued.

Exchange facilities. Money can be changed at banks, bureaux de change and branches of Rennies Travel (Thomas Cook) in St George's Street (tel: 021-423 7154) or at the V&A Waterfront (tel: 021-418 3744). Some hotels also offer an exchange facility, but charge a high commission.

Travellers' cheques and credit cards. Travellers' cheques are accepted by many hotels, restaurants and shops in the city. International credit and debit cards are widely accepted, especially Visa and MasterCard, but also American Express and Diners Club. Cards cannot be used to pay for car fuel at filling stations.

OPENING HOURS

Banks are open 9am–3.30pm Monday–Friday and 9am–11am Saturday, but bureaux de change are generally open until at least 5pm.

Most shops are typically open from 8.30am–5pm Monday–Friday, and until 1pm on Saturday. Supermarkets and many liquor stores tend to close later – around 6pm Monday–Friday and 5pm on Saturday. In the city centre, you will also find many shops open later, and some open on Sunday mornings. Many shops at the V&A Waterfront offer late-night shopping (most until 9pm) seven days a week.

P

POLICE

In an emergency contact the Police Flying Squad: tel: **10111**.

Members of the South African Police are armed, and wear blue uniforms and peaked caps. The growing importance of tourism to South Africa is producing a police force which is more tourist-friendly, but their past role as enforcers of apartheid and more contemporary image as corrupt and uninterested in solving crime mean that they are not greatly respected by many citizens. Even if the police do appear to be less than enthusiastic about solving the crime if you are robbed, you will need to report incidents to them for insurance purposes, and to produce some form of identification when you do so.

POST OFFICES

The main post office in Cape Town is on Parliament Street. Its opening hours are 8am–4.30pm Monday, Tuesday, Thursday and Friday, 8.30am–4.30pm Wednesday and 8am–noon Saturday. Smaller post offices will be closed at lunchtime (1–2pm). Postboxes are painted red.

PUBLIC TRANSPORT

Unlike many other South African cities, Cape Town has reasonable public transport.

Buses. A good bus network operates between the city centre and the V&A Waterfront, Table Mountain, the Southern Suburbs, Kirstenbosch National Botanical Gardens and most popular beaches along the False Bay coast. Buy your ticket from the driver. If you plan to travel by bus a great deal, a Ten Ride Clip Card could save you money.

A number of luxury intercity coach companies operate from Cape Town along the major tourist routes such as the Garden Route. These include Intercape Coaches (tel: 021-380 4400; www.intercape.co.za) and Greyhound (tel: 083-915 9000; www.greyhound.co.za).

Railway. Trains run very frequently at peak times from the city centre through the suburbs to Simon's Town on the False Bay coast. The stations are not signposted, so you will need a map to help you find them. Tickets should be bought in advance from the station, and timetables can be bought at the station or from newsagents.

Taxis. There are three types of taxi available – Rikkis, metered taxis and minibus taxis. Rikkis are a highly tourist-friendly form of transport. You can hail these three-wheeled vehicles from the street or order one by phone (tel: 021-423 4888). They take several passengers, but it is possible to hire one on an exclusive basis for short tours to destinations such as Cape Point.

Metered taxis are available from taxi ranks around the city, or can be ordered by phone. They are not the cheapest form of transport, but at night are the safest alternative to driving yourself.

Minibus taxis are not recommended for tourists. Unlike metered taxis, they can be hailed from the street, but are usually driven recklessly. They are often owned by rival factions, and the drivers generally carry guns.

R

RELIGION

Although the majority of South Africans are Christian, all denominations are represented, and Cape Town has many places of worship, including churches, mosques, temples and synagogues.

T

TELEPHONES

The international dialling code for South Africa is +27. The dialling code for Cape Town is 021 from within South Africa; drop the 0 if calling from abroad. The international access code to dial out of South Africa is 00, followed by the relevant country code.

There are plenty of Telkom public phone booths in Cape Town, from which domestic and international calls may be made. The green public phones use telephone cards, available from post offices, the airport, bookshops and certain supermarkets and hotels. The cards are available in amounts from R10 to R100. International calls from South Africa are cheapest 8pm–8am Monday to Friday and Saturday afternoon through Sunday night.

The directory enquiries service is free, and can be accessed by calling 1023 (domestic numbers) or 0903 (international numbers). Bear in mind that operators may not speak English as their main language, so be prepared to talk slowly and clearly, repeating yourself if necessary.

Mobile phones, operating on the GSM digital system, work well and are extremely common. Travellers bringing their own mobile phones with them should check the roaming agreement with their service provider. Depending on how often you use the phone and where you are most likely to call regularly, it may work out a lot cheaper to buy a South African SIM card to replace the one you use at home for the duration of your stay. The main providers are MTN and Vodacom, and SIM cards can be bought at any of their outlets, as well as at most large supermarket chains.

TICKETS

Tickets for concerts, theatre, opera and ballet performances, and cinemas are bookable through Computicket. You can call them at tel: 021-430 8000 or visit the booth at Victoria Wharf at the V&A Waterfront.

TIME ZONES

Cape Town (and all of South Africa) is two hours ahead of Greenwich Mean Time, seven hours ahead of US Eastern Standard Time year-round and one hour in advance of central European winter time.

TIPPING

Waiters and waitresses should receive 10–15 percent of the bill, unless a service charge is included already. Taxi drivers, bartenders, hairdressers and tour guides also expect to receive 10 percent of the bill. R1–2 per bag is appropriate for hotel porters, and R20 per week for hotel maids. In addition, all petrol stations use attendants, who should be tipped R2–3 for cleaning your windows and checking oil and water.

TOILETS

Good public toilets can usually be found in shopping centres, petrol stations and tourist attractions. Facilities at national parks and beaches may be more basic, but the standard of hygiene is usually high. A small charge is sometimes levied.

TOURIST INFORMATION (see also WEBSITES)

Before your trip, contact the South African Tourist Board branch in your home country, or check the website www.southafrica.net. An excellent network of tourist information offices operate throughout the Western Cape. Every region, however small, has its own tourist board, but remember that many of them are not open on Saturdays.

Australia/NZ: Suite 301, Level 3, 117 York Street, Sydney; tel: +61 2 9261 5000; fax: +61 2 9261 2000; email: info.au@southafrica.net.
US: 500 Fifth Ave, Suite 2040, New York, NY 10110; tel: +1 212 730 2929; fax: +1 212 764 1980; email: info.us@southafrica.net.
UK: 5–6 Alt Grove, London SW19 4DZ; tel: +44 20 8971 9350; fax: +44 20 8944 6705; email: info.uk@southafrica.net.

Also very useful is **Cape Town and Western Cape Tourism**, an official provincial body that operates 86 tourist offices in the province, and has an excellent website with detailed listings and on-line booking facilities, as well as contact details for all offices:
Cape Town and Western Cape Tourism, Pinnacle Building, corner Burg and Castle streets, Cape Town; tel: 021-426 5639/47; fax: 021-426 5640; www.tourismcapetown.co.za.

WEBSITES

It is possible to gather a vast amount of information before you travel. Some useful and informative websites are:

www.tourismcapetown.co.za Official website of Cape Town and Western Cape Tourism.

www.cape-town.org Unofficial site with plenty of good tourist info.

www.discoverthecape.com Another very useful unofficial site.

www.mg.co.za The website of the *Mail & Guardian* newspaper. It contains hundreds of links to other websites of interest.

www.capetown.tv Aimed at gay and lesbian travellers.

www.gardenroute.org.za Garden Route tourism.

www.iziko.org.za Links to many of the museums in the city.

www.waterfront.co.za V&A Waterfront website.

WEIGHTS AND MEASURES

South Africa uses the metric system.

Y

YOUTH HOSTELS

There are many youth hostels and backpackers' lodges in and around Cape Town. Although accommodation is fairly basic, they usually have cafés and communal kitchens, and many offer internet access.

A more upmarket type of backpackers' lodge has also recently started to emerge, offering more comfortable, peaceful accommodation, but still at very low cost (around US$15 per person per night).

There are a host of websites giving links to youth hostels and lodges, including www.hostels.com/za.html and www.coasting africa.com. Hostelling International South Africa (tel: 021-423 8721; www.hisa.org.za) has a number of lodges and hostels in Cape Town and the Western Cape.

Some of the most comfortable include: Ashanti Lodge, 11 Hof Street Gardens, tel: 021-423 8721, www.ashanti.co.za; and The Backpack, 74 New Church Street, Tamboerskloof, tel: 021-423 4530, www.backpackers.co.za.

Recommended Hotels

Cape Town has a wide range of accommodation, so whether you are looking for a hip hang-out or a snug home-from-home with sea views, you will not be disappointed. Most of the big luxury hotels are located in the city centre, on the V&A Waterfront and along the Atlantic seaboard, and are relatively pricey. However, a number of smaller boutique hotels, often with no more than 20 rooms, have sprung up over the last few years in the city centre and such Southern Suburbs as Bishopscourt and Constantia. If you want the best cosmopolitan experience, close to a wide range of restaurants and all the popular beaches, find a place in the city centre or Atlantic seaboard. For a more tranquil environment, head for the Southern Suburbs.

The hotels below are price-graded and all take major credit cards. These prices are based on the average cost of a double room:

$$$$$	over R2,000
$$$$	R1,200 to R2,000
$$$	R800 to R1,200
$$	R400 to R800
$	under R400

IN CAPE TOWN

Breakwater Lodge $$ *Portswood, V&A Waterfront, Cape Town 8002, tel: 021-406 1911, fax: 021-406 1070, www.bwl.co.za.* This former prison is now a budget hotel with a superb location. The rooms are basic but comfortable. Conference facilities. Disabled access. 327 rooms.

The Cape Grace $$$$$ *West Quay, V&A Waterfront, Cape Town 8002, tel: 021-410 7100, fax: 021-419 7622, www.capegrace.com.* Its prime location on the Waterfront, with wonderful views of Table Mountain, make this a much sought-after hotel at the luxury end of the market. Family-owned and a member of the Small Luxury Hotels of the World. Swimming pool, private library, boardroom. Disabled access. 102 rooms.

Cape Heritage Hotel $$$$ *90 Bree Street, Cape Town, tel: 021-424 4646, fax: 086-616 7281, www.capeheritage.co.za.* Modern facilities in an 18th-century house in the heart of the city, close to Heritage Square and the Bo-Kaap. Ideal for exploring the city and for access to shops and restaurants. Gymnasium. 15 rooms.

Daddy Longlegs $$ *134 Long Street, Cape Town, tel: 021-422 3074, www.daddylonglegs.co.za.* One of Cape Town's most talked-about new hotels, Daddy Longlegs consists of a dozen artistically and eccentrically decorated rooms, each with a different theme, and is in a great location for exploring the nightlife around trendy Long Street. It is a real winner, and very reasonably priced, too, but the decor may be too quirky for some tastes.

Four Rosmead Boutique Guesthouse $$$$ *4 Rosmead Road, Oranjezicht, tel: 021-480 3810, fax: 021-423 0044, www.four rosmead.com.* Situated in an upmarket part of the city, this stylish small hotel combines refurbished Victorian architecture with earthy decor featuring contemporary South African artworks, and superb views to Table Bay and Table Mountain. 10 rooms.

iKhaya Guest Lodge $$$ *Dunkley Square, Gardens, Cape Town, tel: 021-461 8880, fax: 086-631 3292, www.ikhayalodge.co.za.* Splendid wood and stone carvings and sandstone walls emphasise the African ambience of this comfortable small lodge in the heart of the historic city centre. 16 rooms, including some self-catering apartments.

The Metropole $$$$ *38 Long Street, Cape Town, tel: 021-424 7247, fax: 021-424 7248, www.metropolehotel.co.za.* This is the latest hip addition to Long Street. Set inside an old Victorian building, the upbeat interiors are Manhattan-glam meets sassy Afro-chic. The M Bar is where you'll find a funky crowd chilling out on comfy red sofas, and the elegant Veranda restaurant offers simple, fusion-style cuisine, Mon–Sat evenings. Downstairs, the M Café serves breakfasts and ready-to-go, lighter deli-style meals and buffet lunches.

The Mount Nelson $$$$$ *76 Orange Street, Cape Town 8000, tel: 021-483 1000, fax: 021-483 1001, www.mountnelson.co.za.*

This gracious landmark, known affectionately as 'the Nellie', is the symbol of elegance and the height of luxury, nestling in the shadow of Table Mountain. From the moment you drive up the palm-fringed avenue to the main entrance you cannot fail to enjoy your stay. Afternoon tea on the terrace is a real treat. An Orient Express hotel and member of the Leading Hotels of the World. Gymnasium, swimming pool, tennis, hair and beauty salon. Disabled access. 226 rooms.

Peninsula All-Suite Hotel $$$–$$$$ *Beach Road, Green Point, tel: 021-430 7777, fax: 021-430 7776, www.peninsula.co.za.* The spacious studios and apartments in this seafront tower block in Green Point are particularly suited to long-stay visitors and families seeking to keep down costs by self-catering. Good facilities include a regular shuttle to V&A Waterfront and an enjoyable swimming pool area. Check online for off-season specials. 110 rooms.

OUTSIDE THE CITY CENTRE

The Bay Hotel $$$$$ *Victoria Road, Camps Bay 8040, tel: 021-438 4444, fax: 021-438 4433, www.thebay.co.za.* All rooms enjoy views of the Atlantic Ocean or the Twelve Apostles and Table Mountain. The hotel overlooks the beach of this trendy resort just 10 minutes from central Cape Town. Member of the Small Luxury Hotels of the World. Swimming pool. 77 rooms.

British Hotel Apartments $$$$ *Simon's Town, tel/fax: 021-786 2214, www.britishhotelapartments.co.za.* Built in 1897, this former hotel has been refurbished and decorated in period style to form a quartet of spacious two-bedroom self-catering apartments. It is good value, and the historic setting is ideal for exploring the rest of the Cape Peninsula in a private vehicle.

The Cellars Hohenort $$$$$ *93 Brommersvlei Road, Constantia 7800, tel: 021-794 2137, fax: 021-794 2149, www.cellars-hohenort. com.* Sister hotel to The Plettenberg (Plettenberg Bay) and The Marine Hotel (Hermanus), this historic Cape Dutch hotel, set in beautiful landscaped gardens bordering Kirstenbosch, is a taste of old-world luxury in the Southern Suburbs. Two swimming pools, tennis court. 56 rooms.

Hout Bay Hideaway $$ *Skaife Street, Hout Bay, tel: 021-790 8040, www.houtbay-hideaway.com.* Blissfully secluded and exclusive, in gorgeous gardens, only a few minutes from the beach and the village. Its suites and apartments are all tastefully furnished; spacious bedrooms with extra-large beds and an eclectic mix of furniture, antique and modern. Has ADSL internet connection, sun-decks, barbecue area and a solar-heated saltwater swimming pool.

Lord Nelson's Inn $$ *St George's Road, Simon's Town, tel: 021-786 3761, fax: 021-789 1009, email: lordnelsoninn@yahoo.co.uk.* This delightful, small but long-serving inn offers unpretentious, homely and very reasonably priced accommodation and meals within walking distance of Boulders Beach and a short drive from the Cape of Good Hope.

Steenberg Country Hotel $$$$$ *Steenberg Estate, Constantia Valley 7945, tel: 021-713 2222, fax: 021-713 2251, www.steenberg hotel.com.* This wine estate dates back to 1682, with rooms in the old Cape Dutch Manor House, the Jonkerhuis and the restored barn, some furnished with antiques. Swimming pool, golf, winery. 19 rooms.

Twelve Apostles Hotel $$$$$ *St George's Road, Camps Bay, tel: 021-437 9000, fax: 021-437 9055, www.12apostleshotel.com.* Opened in 2003, this plush boutique hotel was hot-listed in *Conde Nast Traveller* and *Travel and Leisure*, while *GQ* named it 'Hotel with the Best View in the World' – suffice to say that the food, service and ambience live up to the view.

EXCURSIONS

STELLENBOSCH AND THE WINELANDS

Die Ou Pasterie $$$$ *41 Lourens Street, Somerset West 7130, tel: 021-850 1660, fax: 021-851 3710, www.die-ou-pastorie.com.* A charming guest house adjoining one of the Cape's best restaurants (also called Die Ou Pasterie, *see page 140*), in a relaxing location with good views. Swimming pool, Victorian pub. 16 rooms.

D'Ouwe Werf $$$–$$$$ *30 Church Street, Stellenbosch 7600, tel: 021-887 4608, fax: 021-887 4626, www.ouwewerf.com.* Friendly, helpful staff and good food at this delightfully historic inn in the heart of old Stellenbosch. Shady courtyard for relaxing breakfasts, lunches or teas. Swimming pool. 25 rooms.

Grand Roche $$$$$ *Plantasie Street, Paarl 7622, tel: 021-863 5100, fax: 021-863 2220, www.granderoche.co.za.* Renowned for its famous Bosman's restaurant *(see page 140)*, this luxury hotel is set amongst the vineyards of Paarl. Amenities include gymnasium, two swimming pools, tennis, massage, sauna, steam-room. 35 rooms.

Lanzerac Manor & Winery $$$$ *Lanzerac Road, Stellenbosch 7600, tel: 021-887 1132, fax: 021-887 2310, www.lanzerac.co.za.* One of South Africa's most gracious country hotels, set in its own 300-year-old wine estate; a quiet location at the start of the Jonkershoek Valley. Swimming pool, conference facilities. 40 rooms.

Le Quartier Français $$$$$ *16/18 Huguenot Street, Franschhoek, tel: 021-876 2151, fax: 021-876 3105, www.lqf.co.za.* A hidden gem, set in beautiful and fragrant gardens extending from Franschhoek's most famous restaurant, The Tasting Room *(see page 141)*. Swimming pool, complimentary mini-bar. 17 rooms.

HERMANUS AND THE TIP OF AFRICA

Arniston Hotel $$$$ *Arniston Hotel, Arniston, tel: 028-475 9000, fax: 028-475 9633, www.arnistonhotel.com.* A modern-looking hotel located on the seafront of the beautiful Arniston Bay, a short walk from the harbour and fishermen's cottages. Some rooms with superb view. Friendly, helpful staff make your stay a delight. Disabled access. 30 rooms.

Auberge Burgundy $$$ *16 Harbour Road, Hermanus 7200, tel: 028-313 1201, fax: 028-313 1204, www.auberge.co.za.* Luxury

Provençal-style guest house in the centre of town. Beautiful court-yards and gardens. Swimming pool. 18 rooms.

The Marine Hermanus $$$$$ *Marine Drive, Hermanus 7200, tel: 028-313 1000, fax: 028-313 0160, www.marine-hermanus.co.za.* Sister hotel to The Plettenberg (Plettenberg Bay) and The Cellars Hohenort (Constantia), this luxury hotel on the clifftop is perfect for whale-watching. Swimming pool. 47 rooms.

Whale Rock Lodge $$$ *26 Springfield Avenue, Hermanus 7200, tel: 028-313 0014/5, fax: 028-312 2932, www.whalerock.co.za.* Attractive, small thatched lodge, just a short walk from one of the best whale-watching locations in the area. Swimming pool. 11 rooms.

THE GARDEN ROUTE

Belvidere Manor $$$$ *Belvidere Estate, Knysna 6570, tel: 044-387 1055, fax: 044-387 1059, www.belvidere.co.za.* Relaxing location overlooking Knysna Lagoon and the town. Reception and dining rooms are in the Manor House, but guests stay in cottages, with verandas and fireplaces, in 4 hectares (10 acres) of gardens. Swimming pool. 30 cottages.

Bitou River Lodge $$ *tel/fax: 044-535 9577, www.bitou.co.za.* Voted South Africa's Best B&B/Guest House for three successive years starting in 2003, this luxurious owner-managed guest house consists of just five rooms set along the forested banks of the Bitou River about 10km (6 miles) from Plettenberg Bay.

Fancourt Hotel & Country Club Estate $$$$$ *Montagu Street, Blanco, George 6530, tel: 044-804 0000, fax: 044-804 0700, www.fancourt.co.za.* A golf-lover's paradise on one of South Africa's finest courses. The old manor house at the heart of the hotel is a national monument. Amenities include swimming pools, tennis, bowls, squash, golf. 100 rooms.

Hoogekraal Country House $$$ *P.O. Box 34, George 6530, tel: 044-879 1277, fax: 044-879 1300, www.hoogekraal.co.za.* This former homestead of the Botha family is now a country house hotel where guests stay in the farmhouse rooms, furnished with antiques of the period when each building was erected. Candlelit dinners in the antique-furnished dining room are both entertaining and memorable. Seven rooms.

Hunter's Country House $$$$$ *Pear Tree Farm, Plettenberg Bay 6600, tel: 044-501 1111, fax: 044-501 1100, www.hunterhotels. com.* Luxury country house hotel which offers warm, personalised service of the highest quality. Swimming pool. Member of Relais & Châteaux. 21 garden suites.

Rosenhof Country Lodge $$$$ *264 Baron Van Rheede Street, Oudtshoorn 6620, tel: 044-272 2232, fax: 044-272 3021, www. rosenhof.co.za.* Delightful hotel with rooms opening onto a rose garden. Good food served in dining room of main house. 14 rooms.

WEST COAST

Bushmanskloof Wilderness Reserve $$$$$ *R344, Kenilworth, tel: 021-685 2598, fax: 021-685 5210, www.bushmanskloof.co.za.* This thatched lodge in the Cederberg Mountains offers the chance to experience the beauty of the region, to view its wildlife such as Cape mountain zebra and gemsbok in their natural habitat, and to see some fine examples of Bushman rock art. In spring the valley is carpeted in colourful wild flowers. Member of Relais & Châteaux. Swimming pool. Ten rooms.

Farmhouse Hotel $$–$$$ *5 Egret Street, Langebaan 7357, tel: 022-772 2062, fax: 022-772 1980, www.thefarmhouselangebaan. co.za.* Comfortable accommodation in a mid-19th-century farmhouse close to the West Coast National Marine Park, with views of the stunning Langebaan Lagoon. Swimming pool. 15 rooms.

Kagga Kamma $$$$$ *Near Citrusdal, tel: 021-872 4343, fax: 021-872 4524, www.kaggakamma.co.za.* A private reserve, with craggy scenery, ancient rock art and a San village, offering lodging in luxury chalets or tents, and there is a restaurant and swimming pool.

Recommended Restaurants

Eating out in the Western Cape is a great pleasure, and one that can be enjoyed even on a budget. Dining in South Africa is relatively cheap by European standards and good value even for Americans. The standard of food is generally good, and the cosmopolitan nature of Cape Town means that visitors are spoilt for choice. Below is a selection of restaurants which offer good food, service and, in many cases, a delightful setting. There are lots more, so don't be afraid to look beyond these listings.

In general, staff in cafés and restaurants earn a pittance and are therefore dependent on tips to take home a good wage. As a result, the standard of service tends to be good. A tip of 10 to 15 percent of the cost of the meal is the accepted norm.

The restaurants listed below are price-graded. These prices are based on the average cost of a three-course meal, excluding wine and tips:

$$$$$	over R150
$$$$	R100 to R150
$$$	R75 to R100
$$	R50 to R75
$	under R50

IN CAPE TOWN

Africa Café $$$ *108 Shortmarket Street, Heritage Square, tel: 021-422 0221.* Dinner Monday–Saturday; lunch by arrangement. Excellent buffet of authentic African cuisine, with a useful location in the city bowl.

Aubergine $$$$$ *39 Barnet Street, Gardens, tel: 021-465 4909.* Lunch on weekdays; dinner daily; Sunday dinner only during summer season. Exquisite classical French/Continental cuisine with good selection of vegetarian dishes. Wine-lovers should try the set *dégustation* menu, each course of which comes with a carefully selected Cape wine.

Baia Seafood Restaurant $$$ *V&A Waterfront, tel: 021-421 0935.* Lunch and dinner daily. This lively new restaurant specialises in Portuguese seafood and meat dishes, which can be enjoyed on a wide balcony facing Table Mountain.

Bukhara $$$ *33 Church Street, city centre, tel: 021-424 0000.* Lunch Monday–Saturday; dinner daily. Busy gourmet Indian restaurant with fine food. Vegetarian options. Corkage R20.

Café Bardeli $$ *Longkloof Studios, Darter Street (off Kloof Street), Gardens, tel: 021-423 4444.* Breakfast, lunch, tea and dinner daily. Great place to hang out and relax. Occasional live music.

Cape Colony $$$$$ *Mount Nelson Hotel, city centre, tel: 021-483 1000.* Breakfast, lunch and dinner daily. Wonderful South African food, including Cape Malay dishes, in the grandest old hotel in Cape Town. Vegetarian options. Wines for all tastes. Corkage R20.

Chef Pon's Asian Kitchen $$ *12 Mill Street, Gardens, tel: 021-465 5846.* Lunch and dinner daily. An essential stop for spice junkies, this unpretentious and affordable pan-Asian eatery has a menu that ranges from Japan and China to India and Mongolia.

De Goewerneur $$ *Castle of Good Hope, Darling Street, city centre, tel: 021-461 4895.* Monday–Saturday 9am–4pm. Colonial restaurant serving Cape Malay and international food and snacks inside the Castle. Limited wine list. Dinner for groups by advance arrangement only.

Den Anker Restaurant and Bar $$$ *Pierhead, V&A Waterfront, tel: 021-419 0249.* Lunch and dinner daily. This long-serving waterfront favourite has a great open-air dining area facing the harbour, while the high-ceilinged interior is constructed around a ship-shaped bar. It serves Belgian specialities such as mussels and rabbit, and the wine list is supplemented by a range of imported Belgian beers.

The Green Dolphin Jazz Restaurant $$$ *Victoria and Alfred Mall, Pierhead, V&A Waterfront, tel: 021-421 7471.* Hear some of the best Cape Town jazz around playing every night at this sophisticated bistro which specialises in ostrich meat and seafood. Major credit cards. Entrance R25 on jazz nights.

Hildebrand Restaurant $$ *Pierhead, V&A Waterfront, tel: 021-425 3385.* Lunch and dinner daily. Classic Italian trattoria on the Waterfront. Vegetarian options. Comprehensive wine list plus good selection of cocktails and aperitifs. Corkage R15.

Mesopotamia $$$ *Corner of Long and Church streets, tel: 021-424 4664.* Dinner only daily. The only Kurdish restaurant in South Africa. Recline on floor cushions to eat authentic Kurdish food (the *iskender* – oven-roasted diced lamb with bread, garlic yogurt and tomato sauce – and the *beyti* – minced-chicken kebab rolled in nan bread with garlic yogurt – are delicious). There's tons of atmosphere, with hookah pipes, kelims on the floor and belly dancers to entertain. It's always busy, mostly with a young crowd.

Miller's Thumb $$$ *10B Kloofnek Road, Tamboerskloof, tel: 021-424 3838.* Lunch Tuesday–Friday; dinner Monday–Saturday. Seafood and meat with Creole spicing and other international flavours, in lively contemporary surroundings. Small but well-chosen wine list. Corkage R10.

Noon Gun Tearoom and Restaurant $ *273 Longmarket Street, Signal Hill, tel: 021-424 0529.* Lunch, tea and dinner Monday–Saturday. Tearoom and restaurant which serves Cape Malay food, including halal dishes, at the foot of Signal Hill. Vegetarian options. No alcohol served or permitted.

Ocean Basket $$ *75 Kloof Street, Gardens, tel: 021-422 0322.* Lunch Monday–Saturday. Part of a restaurant chain, this is a great place to eat reasonably priced seafood. Busy and fun. There is also a branch at V&A Waterfront. Limited wine list.

One Waterfront $$$$ *Cape Grace Hotel, V&A Waterfront, tel: 021-418 0520.* Breakfast, lunch, tea and dinner daily. Fine restaurant in five-star hotel formerly voted as the 'best small luxury hotel in the world'. Diners enjoy a wonderful view of Table Mountain. The decor has an African theme, and this is extended to the food. How about milk-poached kingklip, or a curried risotto? Vegetarian options. Excellent and expansive wine list. Corkage R20.

Rozenhof $$$$ *18 Kloof Street, Gardens, tel: 021-424 1968.* Lunch Monday–Friday; dinner Monday–Saturday. Comfortable and informal dining in a historic house with yellowwood ceilings. Good wine list, with many available by the glass. Corkage R12.50.

Savoy Cabbage $$$$ *Heritage Square, city centre, tel: 021-424 2626.* Lunch Monday–Friday; dinner Monday–Saturday. Gracious champagne bar and restaurant with frequently changing menu. Wonderful seafood and many vegetarian dishes. Good selection of well-priced wines. Corkage R20.

OUTSIDE THE CITY CENTRE

Black Marlin $$$ *Main Road, Miller's Point, Simon's Town, tel: 021-786 1621.* Lunch daily; dinner Monday–Saturday. Famous seafood restaurant in an old whaling station. Excellent food and fine views. Good wine list.

Blues $$$$ *The Promenade, Victoria Road, Camps Bay, tel: 021-438 2040.* Lunch and dinner daily. Trendy and fashionable restaurant with appealing menu. Vegetarian options.

Café Pescado $$ *118 St George's Street, Simon's Town, tel: 021-786 2272.* Breakfast, lunch, tea and dinner daily. Seafood any way you like it in a casual environment. Ordinary wine list. Enjoy its good selection of beers. Corkage R10.

Constantia Uitsig $$$$ *Uitsig Farm, Spaanschematriver Road, Constantia, tel: 021-794 4480.* Lunch Tuesday–Sunday; dinner daily; booking essential. Contemporary cuisine with a Mediterranean feel. Excellent seafood. Vegetarian options. Wine list includes best from the Cape and Constantia Uitsig's own label. Corkage R15.

Green House Restaurant $$$$ *The Cellars-Hohenort Hotel, 93 Brommersvlei Road, Constantia, tel: 021-794 2139, www.cellarshohenort.com.* Lunch and dinner daily. This is one of the grandest hotels in the Southern Suburbs, occupying an old private mansion set in a magnificent garden in the heart of Constantia. The Green House faces rolling lawns and serves French-inspired classic food; extensive wine list.

Jonkershuis $$$$ *Groot Constantia Estate, Constantia, tel: 021-794 6255.* A little bit of everything from Cape country in the delightful setting of the Cape's oldest wine estate. Only estate wines. Bring-your-own discouraged. Corkage R15.

La Colombe $$$$ *Uitsig Farm, Spaanschemat River Road, Constantia, tel: 021-794 2390.* Ranked among UK *Restaurant* magazine's list of the world's Top 50 Restaurants for 2006, this elegant restaurant on Constantia Uitsig serves wonderful southern French cuisine accompanied by an excellent wine menu in an airy Cape Dutch building set in pretty Winelands scenery.

Myoga Restaurant $$$$ *Vineyard Hotel, Newlands, tel: 021-683 1520.* Lunch Tuesday–Friday; dinner Monday–Saturday. This replacement for the hotel's Al Jardin Restaurant opened in November 2007 and specialises in Japanese and other Asian dishes served meze style. The hotel grounds are rich in atmosphere and offer marvellous views of the mountain. Cape and imported wines.

Seaforth Beach Bar & Restaurant $$ *Seaforth Beach, tel: 021-786 4810.* Lunch and dinner daily. Situated a few minutes' walk from the Boulders penguin colony, this sensibly priced seafood restaurant has a wide balcony overlooking the beach and serves a good selection of lighter pasta dishes and pizzas.

Two Oceans Restaurant & Snack Bar $$–$$$ *tel: 021-784 9200.* Daily 9am–5pm. This large restaurant in the Cape of Good Hope Nature Reserve is a popular lunch stop thanks to its location, which offers staggering views back across False Bay. It serves a decent selection of seafood and other dishes, and has a lengthy wine list.

STELLENBOSCH AND THE WINELANDS

96 Winery Road $$$$ *Off R44 between Somerset West and Stellenbosch, tel: 021-842 2020.* Lunch daily; dinner Monday–Saturday. Excellent country restaurant offering mix of Cape, Eastern and French influences. Incredible wine list to suit all budgets and walk-in cellar. Corkage R10.

Boschendal Restaurant $$$$ *Groot Drakenstein, tel: 021-870 4274.* Situated on the wine estate of the same name between Stellenbosch and Franschhoek, this offers first-class South African cuisine in elegant Cape Dutch surroundings.

Bosman's $$$$$ *Grande Roche Hotel, Plantasie Street, Paarl, tel: 021-863 5100.* Breakfast, lunch and dinner daily. Africa's only restaurant to achieve Relais Gourmand status offers top-class international cuisine, with special tastings by arrangement. Huge wine list to cater for every taste. Corkage R30.

Decameron $$ *50 Plein Street, Stellenbosch, tel: 021-883 3331.* Lunch and dinner daily. Traditional Italian restaurant with delicious specialities of the house. List of Stellenbosch wines. Corkage R8.50.

Die Ou Pasterie $$$$ *41 Lourens Street, Somerset West, tel: 021-850 1660.* Breakfast daily; lunch Tuesday–Friday; dinner Monday–Saturday. Fine cuisine in an early 19th-century parsonage, with seasonal offerings. Award-winning wine list with suggestions to complement food. Corkage R10.

D'Ouwe Werf $$$ *30 Church Street, Stellenbosch, tel: 021-886 4608.* Breakfast, lunch, tea and dinner daily. Fine food to suit all tastes and appetites in this delightfully welcoming historic inn in the heart of old Stellenbosch. Shady courtyard for relaxing breakfasts, lunches or teas. Wine list offers best of Stellenbosch wines. Corkage R6.

The Tasting Room at Le Quartier Français $$$$$ *16/18 Hugue-not Street, Franschhoek, tel: 021-876 2151.* Dinner daily. The restaurant which established Franschhoek's reputation for fine food was placed among UK *Restaurant* magazine's 50 best restaurants in the world for three successive years starting in 2005. The four-, six- and eight-course menus are very eclectic, and the last is served with a different wine for each dish. Superb wine list.

Terroir $$$$$ *Kleine Zalze Wine Farm, off R44, Stellenbosch, tel: 021-880 8167.* Lunch Tuesday–Sunday; dinner Tuesday–Saturday. An earthy, reed-roofed farmhouse restaurant, with terracotta floor tiles and crisp white linen tablecloths. Chef Michael Broughton's ever-changing menu celebrates seasonal, locally sourced ingredients, elegantly presented and delicious to eat. Excellent quality.

Wijnhuis $$$ *Andringa Street, Stellenbosch, tel: 021-887 5844.* Breakfast, lunch and dinner daily. Essential for all visitors to Stellenbosch. Restaurant/wine bar/wine shop combination makes for a great introduction to the wines of Stellenbosch. Wine-tasting menu changes daily and permits tasting of six wines for next to nothing. Stocks wines from over 40 Stellenbosch estates to buy or drink with the excellent food. Often busy. Corkage R10.

HERMANUS AND THE TIP OF AFRICA

Agulhas Tearoom $$ *In the lighthouse, Agulhas, tel: 028-435 7506.* Lunch Monday–Saturday. Inexpensive light meals and snacks accompanied by a perfect vantage point over the southern tip of Africa.

Arniston Hotel $$$$ *Arniston Hotel, Arniston, tel: 028-475 9000.* Breakfast, lunch and dinner daily. Restaurant with breathtaking view across the harbour and Arniston Bay offers fine food in a friendly environment. The seafood is especially good. Limited list of good wines.

Bientang's Cave $$$$$ *Beachfront, Hermanus, tel: 028-312 3454.* Lunch daily; dinner by arrangement. Seafood served in a cave open to the ocean, reputed to have once been the home of a strandloper woman. Eat inside or out; either way, the location is spectacular. It is not cheap, but few places offer the chance to whale-watch as you enjoy fine food. Opening hours vary, and it is best to call and check. Licensed.

Mogg's Country Cookhouse $$$ *Hemel en Aarde Road, Hermanus, tel: 028-312 4321.* Lunch Wednesday–Sunday; dinner Friday–Saturday. At the end of a gravel road you will receive a warm welcome. Simple farmhouse decor with a rustic menu: casseroles, lamb shanks, venison pie and a few desserts.

THE GARDEN ROUTE

The Copper Pot $$$ *12 Montagu Street, Blanco, George, tel: 044-870 7378.* Lunch Monday–Friday; dinner daily. Founded in 1974, this elegant old house serves delicious French and South African dishes. Excellent wine list to suit all budgets. Corkage R10.

Knysna Oyster Company $$ *Long Street, Thesen's Island, Knysna, tel: 044-382 6942.* Cheap-and-cheerful joint serving oysters cultivated in Knysna Lagoon and the local draught beer.

Phantom Forest Lodge $$$$ *Phantom Pass, near Knysna, tel: 044-386 0046.* Breakfast, lunch and dinner daily. One to be experienced. Hilltop wonderland of bamboo and thatch with treetop plank walkways between buildings. Regularly changing set menu of cuisine from across Africa. Good list of South African wines.

WEST COAST

Die Strandloper $$$ *On the beach, Langebaan, tel: 022-772 2490.* Lunch and dinner daily in summer, call for availability at other times of the year. A not-to-be-missed experience. Ten-course meal including every local seafood you can imagine. Eat as much or as little as you like. Swim or sunbathe between courses. Unlicensed. Cash only.

Evita se Perron $$$ *Darling, tel: 022-492 2851.* Usually dinner Friday–Sunday only. Light snacks with a traditional Cape touch accompany the one-man show performed most weekends by the legendary drag artist and socio-political satirist Pieter Dirk Uys.

INDEX

Adderley Street 28
Afrikaans Taal
  Museum 65
Amphitheatre 39, 87

Bartolomeu Dias
  Museum Complex 71
Baxter Theatre
  Complex 48
Bird Island 80
Bo-Kaap 36–7
Boulders Beach 58

C.P. Nel Museum 74
Cableway 42–3
Cango Caves 75
Cango Wildlife
  Ranch 74
Cape Agulhas 69
Cape Flats 50, 51
Cape of Good Hope
  14, 15, 39, 54, 57, 69
Cape of Good Hope
  Nature Reserve 56–7
Cape Point 43, 54, 57
Castle of Good
  Hope 25–7
Cederberg Wilderness
  Area 80–1
Chapman's Peak
  Drive 56
City Hall 27
Clifton 55
Clock Tower 39
Company's Gardens 15,
  33–4
Constantia 46–7

Da Gama Museum 80
De Hoop Nature
  Reserve 69

De Tuynhuis 32
Diepwalle Forest 75
District Six 27

Fish Hoek 58
Franschhoek 64

Garden Route 70–8
Gold of Africa
  Museum 31–2
Goukamma Nature
  Reserve 72
Government
  Avenue 32–5
Grand Parade 27
Greenmarket Square 30
Groot Constantia 46–7
Groote Kerk 28–9

Harold Porter National
  Botanical Garden 67
Hermanus 66–9
  Old Harbour
    Museum 68
  Shipwreck
    Museum 68
  Whale Crier 68
Holocaust Museum 35
Houses of Parliament 32
Hout Bay 55
Huguenot Memorial
  Museum 64

Irma Stern Museum 48
Iziko Maritime
  Centre 39
Iziko Slave Lodge 29

Kirstenbosch National
  Botanical
  Gardens 44–5

Knysna 75–6
Knysna Elephant
  Park 76
Kommetjie 56
Koopmans de Wet
  House 31
KWV 65

Little Karoo 73–4
Llandudno 55
Long Street 30–1
Long Street Baths 31
Lutheran church 32

Mariner's Wharf 51, 85
Masiphumelele 56
Maynardville Open-Air
  Theatre 50
Mossel Bay 71
Mouille Point
  Lighthouse 55
Mount Nelson Hotel 35
Muizenberg 59

Newlands Cricket and
  Rugby Stadia 49
Noordhoek 56

Old Town House 30
Oudtshoorn 73–4

Paarl 65–6
Planetarium 34
Plettenberg Bay 77
Postberg Nature
  Reserve 80

Red Shed Craft
  Workshop 39
Rhodes Memorial 48–9
Robben Island 51–4

Sendinggestig Missionary
  Meeting House
  Museum 31
Silvermine Nature
  Reserve 59
Simon's Town 58
South African Jewish
  Museum 35
South African Museum
  33–4
South African National
  Gallery 34
South African Naval
  Museum 58
South African Rugby
  Museum 49
Spier 63–4

St George's Cathedral 29
St George's Mall 30
Stellenbosch 62–4
  Oom Samie Se
    Winkel 62–3
  Toy and Miniature
    Museum 63
  Village Museum 63
Storms River
  Mouth 78

Table Mountain 41–3
townships 50, 51
Trafalgar Place Flower
  Market 28
Tsitsikamma National
  Park 78

Two Oceans
  Aquarium 40
University of Cape
  Town 48

Vergelegen Wine
  Estate 66
Victor Verster Prison 65
Victoria and Alfred
  Waterfront 37–40
Victoria Wharf Shopping
  Centre 38

West Coast National
  Park 79–80
Wilderness National
  Park 72

Berlitz pocket guide
Cape Town

Ninth Edition 2008

Written by Karen and Chris Coe
Updated by Philip Briggs
Edited by Anna Tyler
Series Editor: Tony Halliday

Photography credits
Alex Havret 9, 10, 12, 13, 26, 29, 30, 31, 34, 35, 36, 37, 38, 39, 45, 46, 48, 49, 51, 52, 53, 55, 56, 59, 65, 67, 70, 72, 77, 81, 82, 84, 85, 87, 88, 90, 91, 92, 94, 96, 97, 98, 101, 102, 103, 105, 106; Mary Evans Picture Library 16; South African Tourism 6, 14, 21, 42, 57, 60, 62, 69, 74; Bill Wassman 8, 17, 18, 22, 24, 28, 32, 33, 41, 79.

Cover picture: 4 Corners/SIME/Grafenhain Gunter

Printed in Singapore by Insight Print Services (Pte) Ltd, 38 Joo Koon Road, Singapore 628990. Tel: (65) 6865-1600. Fax: (65) 6861-6438

Berlitz Trademark Reg. U.S. Patent Office and other countries. Marca Registrada

Contact us

At Berlitz we strive to keep our guides as accurate and up to date as possible, but if you find anything that has changed, or if you have any suggestions on ways to improve this guide, then we would be delighted to hear from you.

Berlitz Publishing, PO Box 7910, London SE1 1WE, England.
fax: (44) 20 7403 0290
email: berlitz@apaguide.co.uk
www.berlitzpublishing.com